WARRIOR 179

US ARMY GREEN BERET IN AFGHANISTAN 2001–02

LEIGH NEVILLE   ILLUSTRATED BY PETER DENNIS

Series Editor Marcus Cowper

First published in Great Britain in 2016 by Osprey Publishing,
PO Box 883, Oxford, OX1 9PL, UK
PO Box 3985, New York, NY 10185-3985, USA
E-mail: info@ospreypublishing.com

Osprey Publishing, part of Bloomsbury Publishing Plc

A CIP catalogue record for this book is available from the British Library.

ISBN: 978 1 4728 1400 5
E-book ISBN: 978 1 4728 1402 9
PDF ISBN: 978 1 47281 401 2
Editorial by Ilios Publishing Ltd, Oxford, UK (www.iliospublishing.com)

Index by Mark Swift
Typeset in Myriad Pro and Sabon
Artwork by Peter Dennis
Originated by PDQ
Printed in China through World Print Ltd.

16 17 18 19 20 10 9 8 7 6 5 4 3 2 1

www.ospreypublishing.com

DEDICATION

To all current and former US Army Special Forces who have served in Operation *Enduring Freedom* – all gave some, some gave all.

ACKNOWLEDGMENTS

Thanks to my wife Jodi, the US Army Special Forces Association and to Marcus Cowper at Osprey for their support and assistance. Thanks also to JZW for his wonderful images and advice.

ARTIST'S NOTE

Readers may care to note that the original paintings from which the color plates in this book were prepared are available for private sale. The Publishers retain all reproduction copyright whatsoever. All enquiries should be addressed to:

Peter Dennis, Fieldhead, The Park, Mansfield, Notts, NG18 2AT, UK
Email: magie.h@ntlworld.com

The Publishers regret that they can enter into no correspondence upon this matter.

Osprey Publishing supports the Woodland Trust, the UK's leading woodland conservation charity. Between 2014 and 2018 our donations will be spent on their Centenary Woods project in the UK.

MEASUREMENT CONVERSIONS

Imperial measurements are used almost exclusively throughout this book. The exceptions are weapons calibers, which are given in their official designation, whether metric or imperial; and measurements appearing in direct quotes. The following will help in converting imperial measurements to metric.

1 mile = 1.6km
1lb = 0.45kg
1oz = 28g
1 yard = 0.9m
1ft = 0.3m
1in. = 2.54cm/25.4mm
1 gal = 4.5 liters
1 pt = 0.47 liters
1 ton (US) = 0.9 tonnes
1hp = 0.745kW

CONTENTS

US ARMY GREEN BERET IN AFGHANISTAN 2001–02

INTRODUCTION: HISTORY AND TRADITION

The men of the 5th Special Forces Group (Airborne) who famously toppled the Taliban regime in Afghanistan in the latter months of 2001 came from a long tradition of special operations forces (SOF). Their success in Afghanistan owed as much to their history as to their unique skills and uncommon bravery. Green Beret operations in Afghanistan were the proverbial perfect storm, one that felt as if all that had gone before was leading inexorably toward this one campaign in Central Asia.

The United States Army Special Forces were founded in 1952 by Colonel Aaron Bank when he formed the 10th Special Forces Group based on the wartime 1st Special Service Force (SSF), a joint US–Canadian commando unit uniquely qualified in airborne, waterborne and mountain warfare operations. During World War II, the Special Service Force had earned the nickname of the "Devil's Brigade" thanks to its pioneering special operations in Italy and later during the invasion of southern France.

Bank's vision was for a similar Army unit postwar that could operate clandestinely in foreign countries hostile to the United States, conducting unconventional warfare missions and acting as a behind-the-lines force should conventional war ever break out again in Europe. He based his model

A member of a 3rd Special Forces Group ODA (right) and an attached Air Force Combat Controller (left) secure a rooftop during a *shura* (consultation) outside Kabul. Both carry M4A1 SOPMOD carbines with bipods attached. Note the Green Beret wears a commercially purchased Blackhawk Industries load-bearing vest. (USASOC)

A mounted ODA patrol meets villagers as part of a local COIN initiative during early 2002. Note the use of both "clamshell" standard HMMWVs and cargo versions as the Special Force specific variant – the ground mobility vehicle or GMV – was available only in limited numbers. Note also the lack of any form of protective shield for the M240B gunner and the typical baseball cap and Oakleys worn by the gunner. (JZW)

on the capabilities and experiences of the wartime Office of Strategic Services (OSS) and the Jedburgh Teams. The OSS was known for its sabotage missions against German infrastructure targets while the Jedburghs were trained to infiltrate occupied countries undercover to raise and train resistance and guerrilla forces. This new Army Special Forces unit would be a unique mix of the OSS, Jedburghs and the Special Service Force.

The 10th Special Forces Group saw some limited action in Korea, working with North Korean guerrillas but they were otherwise focused on Europe and the crucial stay-behind role should the Soviet Army ever roll across the border into what was then West Germany. One of the Special Forces' lesser-known roles was the deployment of what would now be called "backpack nukes" – the B-54 Special Atomic Demolition Munition – against Soviet armored or headquarters formations. Their primary role however was to raise, train, and advise civilian partisan groups to conduct irregular warfare against occupying Soviet forces.

President Kennedy very actively and publicly supported the Special Forces, seeing them as the ideal warriors for the brush wars and insurgencies that he envisioned to be the new norm as the world powers fought out the Cold War by proxy. The fledgling Special Forces expanded but still concentrated on, and trained for, a number of key roles, including what would become known as Foreign Internal Defense (FID) and Unconventional Warfare (UW), which would eventually become their bread and butter. Simply put, classic Foreign Internal Defense is the task of establishing, training, and mentoring allied nations' militaries to counter an insurgent or guerrilla threat. Unconventional Warfare is sometimes seen as the flip side of the FID coin – in UW, the Special Forces attempt to raise a guerrilla force in a hostile host nation to act against an oppressive regime that is hostile to United States interests.

Kennedy's support of the South Vietnamese government put the Special Forces on the map. They were among some of the earliest American advisers to deploy to Vietnam and they soon became practised exponents of the relatively new doctrine of counter-insurgency. The Special Forces teams focused on villages and hamlets threatened by the Viet Cong (VC). They recruited small local militias against VC infiltration and influence using the concept of the "ink blot" strategy. This was based on developing small ink blots of security around population centers. These ink blots would eventually begin to merge as they multiplied, creating a stable security environment, or so the theory goes.

They were also assigned to the Military Assistance Command Vietnam-Studies and Observation Group (MACV-SOG), a covert long-range reconnaissance unit that often conducted cross-border recon missions deep into North Vietnam and Cambodia. Individual Green Berets were also "sheep-dipped" (placed clandestinely under CIA command) into a CIA program known as Phung Hoang or the Phoenix Program – a controversial operation targeting Viet Cong infrastructure and command and control nodes. The Green Berets were also often deployed as advisers to the CIA's Provincial Reconnaissance Companies – locally raised but US-led militias not dissimilar to the Agency's Counterterrorist Pursuit Teams raised during Operation *Enduring Freedom* (OEF) in Afghanistan some 40 years later.

Post-Vietnam and in the subsequent drawdown of the US military, there were only three active duty but undermanned and under-resourced Special Forces Groups left and their future was seriously in doubt, as were similar allied special operations units such as the British SAS. Burgeoning communist-supported insurgencies in South and Central America and the rapid spread of international terrorism, along with events such as the Soviet intervention into Afghanistan in 1979, saved the Special Forces. The Green Berets were once again the ideal force to counter these new asymmetric conflicts.

During the 1980s, El Salvador in particular became a long-term Foreign Internal Defense effort for the Special Forces. They trained and advised Salvadorian units in Counter-Insurgency (COIN) and Direct Action (DA) tactics. This mentoring played a large part in increasing the capability of the Salvadorian military, allowing it to counter successfully the FMLN insurgency. In Colombia too, Green Beret teams deployed for extended FID missions in support of Colombian military efforts against the FARC narco-terrorists.

When Iraqi dictator Saddam Hussein sent forces to invade Kuwait in August 1990, Special Forces ODAs (Operational Detachment Alphas or simply A-Teams) deployed in support of both Operation *Desert Shield* and the later *Desert Storm*. The ODAs were employed in two of their traditional roles – Foreign Internal Defense embedded with Coalition Arab armies and Special Reconnaissance with a number of small recon teams infiltrating deep into Iraqi-held Kuwait. These missions were institutionally a superb proving ground

AVENGING ANGELS – THE FIRST BOOTS ON THE GROUND
The Green Beret carries the 5.56 x 45mm Special Purpose Rifle (SPR) later designated the Mk 12 Mod 0 and Mod 1 variants. The SPR is fitted with an Ops Inc. sound suppressor, a Leupold LR M3 optic and an early Parker Hale folding bipod. Also shown inset around the Green Beret are the standard BALCS SPEAR combat body armor in US woodland pattern worn by most Special Forces in this time period (**1**); and the AN/PRC-148 Multiband Inter/Intra Team Radio (MBITR) with handset that acts as a line-of-sight radio, allowing communication with aircraft overhead and fellow team members (**2**). Finally, along with the famous shoulder insignia and tabs of the Special Forces (**3**), the inset shows an FDNY (Fire Department New York) patch worn by many Special Forces in memory of the victims of the 9/11 attacks (**4**); an unofficial ODA 555 "Triple Nickel" patch (**5**); and the patches of both Task Force Dagger (**6**) and Task Force K-Bar (**7**)

FIRE DEPARTMENT
CITY OF
NEW YORK

4

SPECIAL FORCES

AIRBORNE

3

TASK FORCE DAGGER
Uzbekistan
STRENGTH and HONOR

6

ODA TRIPLE NICKLE 555

5

2

COMBINED JOINT SPECIAL OPERATIONS
TASK FORCE-SOUTH
TASK FORCE K-BAR

7

1

for their operations in Afghanistan ten years later. They demonstrated that the Green Berets were not just for insurgencies but could also operate alongside conventional forces in a largely conventional warfighting environment.

After the Gulf War, Green Beret ODAs saw action in the Balkans and Somalia, along with a large number of long-term training commitments across the world. These training team missions have expanded and continue today with the Special Forces at the forefront of this vital element of the "war on terror" – developing allied militaries to counter jihadist insurgencies effectively, particularly in Trans Saharan Africa and Central Asia. It is this unique blend of skills that brought Army Special Forces to the fore in the wake of the devastating terrorist attacks on the American homeland of September 11, 2001 and the resulting Operation *Enduring Freedom* in Afghanistan.

RECRUITMENT AND SELECTION: BECOMING A MODERN GREEN BERET; THE Q COURSE AND ROBIN SAGE

Selecting and training Special Forces candidates was conducted by the 1st Special Warfare Training Group at the John F. Kennedy Special Warfare Center and School at Fort Bragg in North Carolina. The selection process itself was conducted in the sandy hills and pine forests of Camp Mackall, a former airborne training site on the sprawling Fort Bragg base, which dates from World War II. This overview of recruitment and selection is based on the procedures used during much of the 1990s, the period in which many of the Green Berets, who later served in Afghanistan in 2001 and 2002, earned their tabs and distinctive headgear.

Candidates for the Special Forces were normally expected to have served a number of years in the Army and have completed Airborne (parachute) School before being accepted into the Special Forces Assessment and Selection (SFAS) course, which served as a pre-selection to filter potential Green Berets. Special Forces soldiers are known as "triple volunteers" as they have volunteered for the Army, then the Airborne and finally for Special Forces. Many candidates have volunteered a fourth time – for the Rangers, and many are recruited directly from the 75th Ranger Regiment.

SFAS was a 24-day selection program that attempted to identify those that the instructors – all seasoned special operators themselves – believed had what it took to qualify as Army Special Forces and win the coveted Green Beret. Timed land navigation exercises (including a 47-mile individual navigation course carrying over 100 pounds in their packs to be completed within a 72-hour time period), route marches, obstacle courses, and other grueling physical tests were only one part of SFAS.

US Army Colonel John Mulholland, commander of the 5th Special Forces Group and Joint Special Operations Task Force-North (better known as Task Force Dagger), hosts then Secretary of Defense Donald H. Rumsfeld at K2 in Uzbekistan in 2001. (DOD photograph by Helene C. Stikkel)

Equally if not more important for future Green Berets were the Situational Awareness Reaction Exercises. These were designed to test how a candidate could think on his feet, adapt to new situations, relate to others and operate as part of a team. All of the scenarios were based on real-world situations ODAs had encountered on operations overseas. According to historian Dick Couch, on average over 3,000 soldiers applied for SFAS each year. Only 600 made the grade to pass onto the second stage of selection – the Special Forces Qualification Course (SFQC).

A 3rd Special Forces Group ground mobility vehicle equipped with both pintle roof-mounted and passenger-side swing-arm-mounted M240B machine guns. Several M136 (AT4) anti-tank rockets are secured to the roof. (USASOC)

Known as the Q Course, SFQC comprised five fixed phases of training that took, in total, from between one to two years to complete (a sixth much shorter administration phase existed – the awarding of the Green Beret to successful candidates and the paperwork of assigning the successful graduate to a Special Forces Group). The exact phasing of the SFQC has changed over the years – for instance at the time of writing, language training had been introduced after the completion of Robin Sage (the final field exercise), but the following phasing was correct for much of the 1990s.

The first phase was the seven-week-long orientation course that gave candidates a thorough understanding of the history, traditions, roles, and planning processes of the Green Berets. Phase two was language, which could last between 18 and 25 weeks, dependent on the language required (for the 5th Special Forces Group, the first into Afghanistan, Arabic and later Pashto were common and are among the more difficult to learn).

The third phase of the Q Course covered small unit tactics and the famously tough SERE (Survival-Evasion-Resistance-Escape) School. Small unit tactics were familiar to many of the candidates from the Rangers and taught high-level infantry skills in building clearance and close-quarter battle (CQB), raiding, ambushing, reconnaissance, patrolling, and advanced marksmanship with all basic Special Forces small arms.

SERE was a three-week training course designed to equip candidates with the skills necessary to survive in the wilderness and evade capture by enemy forces. It was where Special Forces earned their unusual moniker of "snake eaters." The program was created by a Green Beret former prisoner of the North Vietnamese and included a grueling, five-day resistance-to-interrogation module known innocuously as the Resistance Training Laboratory. Similar to a program run by the British SAS, soldiers were held in harsh prison camp conditions, based on the experiences of special operations soldiers that had been held captive in Korea, Vietnam, *Desert Storm* and Somalia. The candidates were taught techniques to resist interrogation and torture which would allow enough time for a Special Forces headquarters to alter operational plans, radio encryption and similar classified materials, and extract any survivors of a compromised patrol.

Phase four of the Q Course consisted of individual Special Forces MOS (Military Occupational Specialty) training. Each soldier was trained in one of the core specialties:

- Weapons – 18 Bravo (three months' duration);
- Engineering – 18 Charlie (three months' duration);
- Medical – 18 Delta (six months' duration);
- Communication – 18 Echo (six months' duration).

Team leaders attended their own MOS School, which covered the entire spectrum of Special Forces missions so that the detachment leaders would have a broad understanding of all of the MOSs of their team and their operational capabilities and limitations. Upon completion of their MOS training, the soldier was considered an expert in his particular specialist field and would eventually become either the senior or junior sergeant in that specialty within his assigned Operational Detachment Alpha.

18 Bravo Weapons Sergeants were, as the name suggests, responsible for the provision and maintenance, and training of local forces in the use of, a massive range of both American-issue and foreign weapons ranging from 9mm pistols to 81mm mortars. The weapons sergeants would be called upon to instruct indigenous forces, often in a language other than English, in everything from core marksmanship principles to basic close-quarter battle techniques. Training Afghan Militia Forces (AMF) in weapons usage would prove particularly challenging, as the Afghans had never received any formal small-arms instruction and had a tendency to fire their AK47s on full automatic in the general direction of the enemy. As the ODAs would later learn, combat in Afghanistan was more an exercise in bravado and intimidation than polished tactical skills.

The 18 Charlie engineering sergeants became masters in how to build things and then how to blow them up. Their MOS course gave them a unique set of skills that drew on civil as well as military engineering. The engineering sergeants would be crucial in any unconventional warfare or foreign internal defense scenario – in Afghanistan, they would be responsible for sinking new wells and building schoolhouses and medical clinics for the local villages. Just as importantly they would also be responsible for supervising the construction of fortified patrol bases (PBs) for the ODAs and their Afghan allies.

Candidates on the final exercise component of the Q Course, Robin Sage, dressed in sterile BDUs. On the exercise, they must support fictional G-Chiefs and their guerrilla army. (USASOC)

The 18 Delta medical sergeants attended the Joint Special Operations Medical Training Center for a 12-month program that initially certified them as combat medics (the equivalent of a civilian paramedic or Emergency Medical Technician) and then trained them in a range of advanced battlefield surgical skills. They also received instruction in a bewildering number of specialist medical subjects including parasitology, diseases, veterinary skills, and even basic dental procedures. The program also included the controversial live tissue trauma training in which pigs and goats were deeply anaesthetized before being subjected to realistic battlefield wounds. The trainee Special Forces medics then had to treat them (these animals were later euthanized without having regained consciousness). In Afghanistan, 18 Delta would soon be treating human casualties, both Afghan and American.

A Special Forces soldier on a Polaris ATV, deployed as part of a sensitive site exploitation (SSE) mission, investigates a cave for munitions caches. (USAF photograph by Senior Airman Bethann Hunt)

Finally the 18 Echo communications sergeants were trained in all manner of modern communications technology from secure e-mail to encrypted burst transmission radios. The communications sergeants trained specifically on the AN/PSC-5 Spitfire UHF and VHF manpack radio, the AN/PRC-137 high frequency radio, the AN/PRC-119 FM radio and the handheld AN/PRC-148 MBITR inter-team radio that is carried by all Special Forces soldiers. They were also trained to use civilian technologies such as the Iridium satellite telephone that proved a useful backup in Afghanistan.

Phase five was the final part of the Q Course and built upon everything the candidate had been taught over the preceding months. It was known as Robin Sage. This component was a fully immersive, five-week-long field exercise in which prospective Green Berets operated in ODA-style teams to work alongside guerrillas (played by Special Forces soldiers) in an extremely realistic Unconventional Warfare scenario. Set in the fictional nation of Pineland, Robin Sage was named after both a nearby town (Robins) and the surname of the Special Forces officer who first established the exercise (Colonel Jerry Sage, a former OSS and 10th Group veteran).

During Robin Sage, the prospective Green Berets had to contact a fictional "G-Chief" or local-national guerilla chief, forge a workable alliance and then train, mentor and support the guerrilla role-players as they joined the fight to liberate Pineland from their fictional oppressors. Robin Sage was eerily prescient of the role Army Special Forces played in Afghanistan and graphically demonstrated why the Green Berets later became the weapon of choice in the campaign. Robin Sage included the use of numerous civilian role-players and for many years local law enforcement, although the tragic shooting of two soldiers – one fatally – during a Robin Sage in 2002 by a nervous sheriff's deputy, who was unaware of the exercise, put an end to civilian police involvement.

After the successful completion of the Q Course, soldiers were awarded the iconic headgear and Special Forces shoulder tabs at a formal mess ceremony before being finally assigned to their first Special Forces Group (most stayed with the team they were initially assigned to – sometimes for the rest of their military careers).

Each Special Forces Company had a team role in which they specialized. These were military free fall parachuting (HALO or High Altitude, Low Opening); combat diving/SCUBA (Self Contained Underwater Breathing Apparatus); mountain warfare; mobility (vehicles); or MOUT (Military Operations in Urban Terrain). Depending on his Company assignment, the newly posted Special Forces soldier might have been sent to a number of schools to prepare him for the team role. He would also have received further advanced training in both military and cultural skills, with advanced language proficiency particularly prized.

It has been claimed that there is no such thing as a fully trained Green Beret. When not deployed, Special Forces are often posted to an incredibly wide range of both military and civilian courses, including the now renamed Special Operations Target Interdiction Course (sniping), various CQB schools, demolitions and breaching training, the Joint Tactical Air Control (JTAC) course and further professional development in their Special Forces MOS, which often includes two-year postings to allied military units including the British and Australian SAS.

This selection and training process develops the skills and maturity that set the Green Berets apart from other special operations forces (SOF). When he is assigned to an ODA, a Green Beret is already a sergeant and is typically in his late twenties or early thirties, much older than most Rangers or SEALs. He will have usually spent more time in the military before applying to SFAS, giving him a level of maturity and worldliness beyond most other SOF – attributes that greatly assist when dealing with third-world guerrillas of questionable provenance in places like Afghanistan or Iraq.

The five doctrinal Special Forces missions[1] – Foreign Internal Defense (FID), Counterterrorism (CT), Unconventional Warfare (UW), Special Reconnaissance (SR), and Direct Action (DA) – make Green Berets a unique combination in the world of SOF. Army Special Forces may be the ultimate exponents of the "Three Block War" concept of modern asymmetric warfare. This theory, developed before the wars in Afghanistan or Iraq, posited that on one city block soldiers might be providing humanitarian support to civilians. On the next block, they might be engaged in counter-insurgency peacekeeping, before, on the final block, being exposed to open, largely conventional warfighting.

1 Since 2001, a number of other non-core missions have been added to the five core missions including Counter-insurgency, Information Operations and Civil Affairs Operations.

B

PINELAND – LEARNING TO EAT SOUP WITH A KNIFE

This scene is typical of the final Robin Sage field exercise that prepares Special Forces soldiers to infiltrate a foreign country clandestinely, make contact with a guerrilla organization and mentor and train them to overthrow a hostile government. Robin Sage was remarkably prescient of the operations that the Green Berets would be eventually called upon to conduct in Afghanistan. This image shows a Robin Sage participant using a sand table model to brief the "freedom fighters" of "Pineland," the fictional nation that is the setting of this final element of the Special Forces Qualification Course, on an upcoming operation. Note the guerrilla role-players are dressed in a mix of civilian and military clothing along with various pieces of wet-weather gear. They also carry a range of Warsaw Pact small arms, better to impersonate the "average" guerrilla Special Forces they will likely work alongside during future operations.

The iconic image from the Afghan war – the "horse soldiers" of ODA 555 riding into battle alongside warlord Fahim Khan's militia. (USASOC)

These five core missions are officially described by the United States Army Special Operations Command (USASOC) thus:

FOREIGN INTERNAL DEFENSE (FID)

These missions are launched when a foreign nation requests help to end lawlessness or protect itself from rogue enemy nations during war or peace. Special Forces organize, assist, and train foreign militaries in protecting their citizens.

COUNTERTERRORISM (CT)

Special Forces conduct offensive strikes to prevent, deter, pre-empt, and respond to terrorism. The covert capabilities of Special Forces Soldiers allow them to conduct these missions in areas where conventional forces cannot operate.

UNCONVENTIONAL WARFARE (UW)

Special Forces Soldiers are experts in guerrilla warfare, as well as training foreign resistance forces in the tactics of subversion, sabotage, intelligence collection and unconventional recovery. A typical UW mission can last months or even years. Additionally, these missions allow conventional US forces to enter a country covertly and build relationships with the local populace.

SPECIAL RECONNAISSANCE (SR)

Before conventional US Army forces strike an enemy, Special Forces are often sent in behind enemy lines to assess troop and weapons strengths and overall operations. These covert, fact-finding operations uncover needed information about the enemy. The success of the follow-on conventional force is often contingent on these missions.

DIRECT ACTION (DA)

DA missions are quick-duration strikes to seize, capture, recover, or destroy enemy weapons and information or to recover designated personnel or material. Other purposes of DA missions include removing an enemy that is gaining power and influence in a foreign nation, and protecting American nationals or Soldiers held in foreign countries.

It is this combination of roles and skills that makes US Army Special Forces unique. At the outset of OEF in Afghanistan, the US Navy SEALs had long concentrated on Special Reconnaissance and Direct Action missions; Marine special operations had traditionally been heavily focused on Special Reconnaissance, and the Army Rangers were still primarily a Direct Action force of elite light infantry with a core mission to seize enemy-held airfields.

Many of these organizations have since embraced Foreign Internal Defense and Unconventional Warfare after many long years of counter-insurgency in Iraq and Afghanistan. In 2001 however, there was simply no other unit with the unique set of capabilities of the Army Special Forces in the US military ready to deploy covertly into Afghanistan.

APPEARANCE: BEARDS AND BASEBALL CAPS

The Green Berets that fought in the early days of the Afghan campaign established a distinctive look that has become widely emulated among both SOF and conventional units. Special Forces doctrine teaches the special operator to blend in with his environment, both for security reasons (to avoid standing out as an American soldier as he is often deploying covertly) and for cultural reasons to ease assimilation with the local forces he is working alongside. In the case of Afghanistan, this meant beards.

In male-dominated Afghan culture, and particularly within the southern Pashtun population, facial hair is considered a necessary rite of passage for adult males, and any man without a beard is not taken particularly seriously. The Green Berets of the 5th Special Forces Group, through their advanced

A Green Beret securing a Taliban munitions cache. Note he wears the typical Polartec SPEAR ECW jacket, ball cap and three-color desert BDU trousers. His weapon is an M4A1 mounting an ACOG optical sight and KAC forward grip. (JZW)

A Special Forces soldier mans a jury-rigged M240B in the rear bed of a US-purchased Toyota Tacoma. The M240B retains its bipod and sling to allow dismounted use. (JZW)

cultural training, understood this and began growing their beards as soon as they were earmarked for an Afghan deployment. A number of SOF units were permitted what was termed relaxed grooming standards, as these units were required to operate covertly or sometimes completely undercover in foreign countries, under Title 10 of the United States Code governing overseas deployment of its armed forces.

During the initial phases of OEF in Afghanistan, the ODAs were operating under Title 10. This allows US military units to operate clandestinely or in secret but with the proviso that no effort is made to conceal the fact that any such clandestine operation has been conducted by United States personnel. The CIA Special Activities Division teams that were the first into Afghanistan conversely operated under Title 50 of the Code that allows for covert operations using sterile weapons, clothing, and equipment, disguising the fact that an operation was being carried out by Americans.

Although permitted by the Army, the relaxed grooming standards policy was inconsistently and sometimes arbitrarily applied – many Green Berets claimed that the number and length of beards grown by an ODA was in direct correlation to the proximity of "Big Army" staff officers. This was not such an issue in the first few months of the war but as conventional forces began to arrive in Afghanistan, the beards became something more contentious.[2]

Ridiculous conditions were attached to the policy, such as, if a bearded Special Forces soldier was at Bagram Air Base for longer than a 24-hour period, he was required to shave, no matter that the beard might have taken months to grow. Being Green Berets, numerous unconventional tactics were soon developed to avoid these restrictions. Non-governmental organizations (NGOs) also complained about Special Forces wearing civilian garb and sporting beards, as they believed it blurred the line between combatant and non-combatant leading to insurgent attacks on NGOs. In reality NGOs were targeted because their work was seen as a threat to Taliban dominance, not because they were mistaken for SOF.

Along with the beards, the Green Berets wore a mixture of civilian attire and Army issue clothing. The first ODAs into Afghanistan wore mainly civilian cargo trousers, flannelette hiking shirts and fleece jackets. Many also sported tan photographer's vests that allowed them to conceal magazines for their M4A1s and pistols without having to wear traditional webbing and magazine pouches.

Later, unless on Special Reconnaissance taskings when dressing in the

2 In late 2002, the Army attempted to "re-adapt uniform and grooming standards" for the Special Forces deployed to Afghanistan with little long-term success as saner minds eventually prevailed. A further 2010 edict all but banned the wearing of beards within SOF assigned to training and advisory missions with Afghan security forces, along with the wearing of non-issue clothing. ODAs operating alongside partnered local forces were advised to shave their beards and to replace their baseball caps with the Afghan *pakol*.

local *shalwar kameez* (the traditional matching baggy top and trousers worn by most Afghan males) was often a distinct tactical advantage, the Green Berets generally wore the then-issue three-color Desert Camouflage Uniform (DCU). The DCUs were worn with desert or civilian hiking boots and fleece jackets and cold-weather gear from a number of civilian outdoor suppliers such as North Face and Helly Hansen. Sometimes, a blanket-like Afghan shawl was worn against the cold.

A black SOCOM (Special Operations Command) issue fleece jacket called the SPEAR Extreme Cold Weather jacket manufactured by Polartec was also extremely popular and was an early distinctive item of Special Forces clothing. Another common feature of all early ODAs was the ubiquitous Oakley sunglasses – most commonly the Oakley M Frame model. These became something of a defining feature of the Green Berets – along with their beards and mix of civilian and issue clothing.

Helmets were considered overly aggressive for counter-insurgency operations (not to mention distinctly marking the wearer as American as no Afghans wore helmets), so instead the Afghan *pakol* flat cap or a civilian baseball cap was often worn. Incredibly, the early Green Beret teams wore no body armor at all for much of their deployment as they felt that, to connect with the Afghan militias, they needed to share the risk with them. Body armor was worn later, either the issue Ceradyne SPEAR/BALCS types or unit-purchased plate carriers manufactured by the likes of Eagle or Blackhawk. The only time when helmets and body armor were consistently worn was on Direct Action missions when the risk of close-range contact with the enemy was high (for instance if raiding a Taliban leader's compound).

As for physical appearance, Special Forces men are older and, although superbly fit, are for the most part not the mountains of muscle popular fiction portrays them as. The average age of the Green Beret in Afghanistan was 32.

The famous ODA 574, pictured with future Afghan President Hamid Karzai, a few minutes before an errant GPS-guided bomb landed nearby, tragically killing three of the Green Berets and seriously wounding several more. Note the mix of Polartec and civilian purchase jackets, Harley Davidson and Oakley baseball caps and green Nomex flight gloves worn by several of the operators. (USASOC)

As previously mentioned, most Rangers and SEALs were in their twenties. Green Berets are closer in age bracket to the special mission units such as Delta Force, giving them a certain physical gravitas when operating alongside Afghan forces. Along with their age, Green Berets tend not to aspire to the body-building physiques seen in some other SOF units such as the SEALs. In common with his counterpart in the British SAS, the average Green Beret is built more for endurance than for physical bulk.

EQUIPMENT AND WEAPONS

The ODAs deploying to Afghanistan took with them a range of weapons that would allow them to adapt to the largely unknown tactical environment on the ground. The most common weapon was the standard-issue M4A1 carbine. A compact modified version of the regular Army's M16A2, the M4A1 fired the 5.56 x 45mm intermediate NATO round and differed only from the Army issue M4 in that it featured a fully automatic selector (Safe-Semi-Auto) rather than burst fire and a heavier-weight barrel to cope with the increased pressure of fully automatic fire.

The ODAs' carbines benefited from a then-new program called the Special Operations Peculiar Modification (SOPMOD) Block I Kit. A number of these SOPMOD kits were allocated to each ODA and contained a range of accessories such as the Trijicon ACOG (four-power magnified optic) and Reflex and Aimpoint sights (non-magnified, close-quarter battle optics); AN/PEQ-2 infrared laser illuminators and Picatinny rails for mounting these items to the carbine (these replaced the standard forearm and provided a common mounting platform for sights, lights and lasers). A common field modification not found in the SOPMOD kits was the addition of several rubber bands to the M4A1's collapsible stock to hold it in the desired position, as the early stocks had a tendency to close up when fired.

Each ODA would be equipped primarily with these M4A1 SOPMOD carbines with at least two also mounting 40mm M203 under-barrel grenade launchers. The M203 provided an indirect fire capability and could launch a range of high-explosive, light-armor penetrating, illumination and smoke rounds. Some teams also packed examples of the veteran Vietnam-era 40mm M79; a stand-alone, single-shot grenade launcher that many claimed was more accurate than its replacement, the M203.

Close personal protection was provided by the regular Army issue 9mm Beretta M9, although some .45ACP M1911A1 pistols were also carried. A number of 9mm Heckler and Koch submachine guns, including both the collapsible stock MP5A3 and the suppressed MP5SD3 models, were also deployed but rarely used, as the 9mm round simply could not compete with the 5.56mm for range or stopping

ODA 585 in northern Afghanistan pictured carrying a mix of M4A1 SOPMOD carbines including at least one mounting an M203 grenade launcher and several equipped with sound suppressors. The suppressed, scoped rifle to the left is the 5.56mm Special Purpose Rifle, later rechristened the Mk 12 Mod 0. (USASOC)

power. In comparison, the CIA SAD teams carried deniable weapons – folding stock AKM assault rifles and 9mm Browning Hi-Power pistols – all without serial numbers from sterile stocks.

From their reading of previous actions during the Soviet–Afghan War, the ODAs knew that they might be involved in some longer-range engagements that would stretch the capabilities of the 5.56mm round fired from their carbines. The small round, coupled with the short barrels of the carbine – which made them excellent for clearing buildings or operating in vehicles – and the type of bullets then being issued (which were not specifically designed to be fired from such short barrels), meant that the M4A1 had an effective range of only several hundred yards.

A cargo HMMWV is pressed into service in eastern Afghanistan by a Green Beret team. The HMMWVs were often too wide to negotiate the mountain trails, forcing the teams to use Toyota pick-up trucks. (JZW)

To cover the distance between their carbines and dedicated sniper rifles such as the M24, the ODAs carried two then-recently issued marksman's rifles into battle: the Mk 11 Mod 0 and what was then known as the Special Purpose Rifle (SPR) and which would eventually be type classified as the Mk 12 Mod 0. The SPR was an outgrowth of a SEAL requirement for a compact, selective fire 5.56mm rifle with a 16-inch barrel to cope with longer-range shooting out to 550 yards, well beyond the capabilities of the M4A1. The SPR also commonly featured a sound suppressor (silencer) to muffle the report of the rifle, if not the supersonic crack of the bullet. Tactically this helped conceal the location from which the shots were being fired.

The Mk 11 was based on the Knight Armament Corporation's (KAC) semi-automatic 7.62mm SR-25. The Mk 11 could accurately engage targets out beyond 550 yards and up to half a mile or more in the right conditions. It was fitted with a Leupold variable power scope and issued with match grade M118LR ammunition. Many of these Mk 11 rifles also featured detachable Ops Inc. sound suppressors and Parker-Hale and later Harris bipods.

For ranges beyond the capabilities of the Mk 11 and SPR, the 7.62 x 51mm M24 sniper rifles, along with the .50 M82A1 Barrett anti-material rifle (later adopted as the M107 by the rest of the US military) were also shipped to Afghanistan. The M24 was a bolt-action rifle based on the commercial Remington 700. It could reliably engage targets at a distance of a half to two-thirds of a mile, again depending on environmental conditions. The M82A1 was a huge semi-automatic anti-material rifle intended for extremely long-range shooting with a stated effective range of just over a mile – although shots have since been made at an incredible distance of nearly two miles with the weapon – firing a match grade version of the massive .50-cal round. Apparently, several commercial heavy-caliber rifles were also employed including the Beowulf .50 and the CheyTac .408.

For providing suppressive fire, the ODAs deployed with the 5.56mm M249 Squad Automatic Weapon (SAW) in both its standard and compact Para version. The SAW fired from a 200-round box magazine out to 750 yards – the Para version's range was considerably shorter owing to its reduced barrel length. Some examples of the M249 Special Purpose Weapon variant were also deployed, which featured a slightly longer barrel than the Para and Picatinny rails and was the precursor of the later Mk 46 version developed specifically for SOCOM.

The heaviest firearm commonly employed by the Green Berets was another machine gun – the belt-fed 7.62mm M240B medium machine gun based on the famous Fabrique Nationale MAG58. Firing from disintegrating link belts, the M240B was a superb suppressive fire weapon, reaching area targets out to 1,100 yards using its bipod. Beyond the M240, the ODAs also took with them the M136 (AT-4) light anti-tank rocket and the venerable Carl Gustav 84mm recoilless rifle. Both proved adept at demolishing Taliban bunkers and cave entrances.

Perhaps the Special Forces' most important weapons were their radios. A range of communications equipment was carried, from the handheld PRC-148 MBITR that could be used to talk to line-of-sight units and aircraft overhead to the sophisticated PRC-137 SATCOM set that could be used to speak directly to CENTCOM headquarters half a world away. Operating alongside these radios was the AN/PSN-11 Precision Lightweight GPS

OFF-ROAD AND UNDERCOVER IN AFGHANISTAN

Perhaps the most iconic image of the Green Beret in Afghanistan, beside that of the operators on horseback, was the Toyota pick-up truck. Various models of Toyota Hilux and Tacoma were purchased either in theatre or modified and shipped from the United States. These Non Standard Tactical Vehicles provided a number of advantages – parts were far more easily obtained than for military vehicles, an important consideration for ODAs working far from normal logistics channels; they fitted into their environment far more covertly than a GMV, and at a distance could be mistaken for an insurgent or civilian vehicle; and they could go places the heavier GMV and HMMWV variants could not, particularly in the mountainous east.

This example is a V6 petrol-driven, dual-cab Toyota Tacoma (**1**). Most of the modifications made to the vehicle are difficult to spot – the antennae for dual band and satellite comms, the self-recovery winch and the Mk19 40mm automatic grenade launcher are far more obvious. Inside the truck, a Blue Force Tracker has been installed allowing real-time tracking and interaction with friendly units along with plotting enemy locations; radio sets have been mounted; all white lights both internally and externally, including the headlights, have been replaced with infra-red or low-light versions. The bed of the truck contains MRE (Meal Ready to Eat) ration packs, drinking water, extra ammunition and an American flag serving as a de-facto IFF (Identification Friend or Foe) marking device (normally a bright orange VS-17 panel is used for this purpose).

Also illustrated are the standard-issue Modular Integrated Communications Helmet (MICH) ballistic helmet with night vision goggle mounting bracket (**2**). The MICH was developed specifically for SOCOM units to improve both ballistic and bump protection and to allow the use of communications headsets with the helmet. A modified version of this helmet later became regular US Army issue Advanced Combat Helmet.

Next to the MICH helmet is the standard-issue US Army fragmentation grenade, the M67 (**3**). With a 15m casualty-producing radius, the M67 comes standard with a four second fuse and an additional safety device keeping the grenade's pin in place following a number of training accidents. Most SF soldiers would carry three to four M67s and several coloured smoke or White Phosphorous grenades.

Finally, below the Tacoma, is shown the issue 9 x 19mm M9 Beretta pistol, often carried by the ODAs as an emergency back-up should their primary weapon fail (**4**). Forced by the terms of The Hague Declaration of 1899 to issue non-expanding rounds, many feel the 9 x 19mm M9 is fatally compromised by its reliance on Hague-legal ball or Full Metal Jacket rounds. These are typically poor at incapacitating an enemy, often overpenetrating the target and creating a small permanent wound channel. Unless on certain counter-terrorism missions, Special Forces soldiers are restricted from using modern hollowpoint or expanding ammunition, although recent news of the proposed Modular Handgun System requirement for the US Army mentions options for the fielding of new bullet designs that may increase the terminal effects of whatever pistol is eventually chosen to replace the venerable M9.

Receiver (PLGR) that could be used to transmit GPS locations. These GPS locations could be plotted on the Falcon View mapping software that the Green Berets had loaded on their Toshiba Toughbook laptops.

As GPS-guided aerial bombs were still in their infancy in 2001, the ODAs also carried a device that could mark targets with an invisible laser beam that was then used to vector in laser-guided bombs; the AN/PEQ-1 Special Operations Forces Laser Acquisition Marker or SOFLAM. The SOFLAM looked like an oversized pair of binoculars and was often seen mounted on a tripod. It could designate targets at ranges between 200 yards and 6 miles, dependent on weather conditions, and became a vital tool for the Special Forces in Afghanistan.

Many of the aircraft tasked with providing close air support were at that time not equipped with targeting pods able to identify, track, and engage small groups of enemy individuals or at best a single enemy SUV. As had been pioneered by A-10As during Operation *Desert Storm* ten years earlier, some pilots attempted to use the camera on the AGM-65 Maverick anti-tank missile as a field expedient targeting pod, but with little success. This was one of the reasons the SOFLAM was so important, as was a competent ground Forward

An Air Force Combat Controller supporting a Special Forces ODA. He carries a SOPMOD M4A1 and wears SPEAR BALCS body armor with pouches attached directly to the vest via MOLLE attachment points. (USAF photograph by Staff Sergeant Jeremy T. Lock)

Air Controller (FAC) to talk in air strikes by guiding the pilot using visible landmarks. With the SOFLAM, a laser-guided bomb should, theoretically, ride the laser beam unerringly to its eventual target.

The ODAs also carried some other high-tech equipment in the form of the HIDRAH Handheld Integrated Directional Receiver and Homing System, which could be mounted on the top of an M4A1's receiver and provided a tactical signals intelligence capability to the ODAs. The HIDRAH was used to track the location of radio signals from Taliban and al-Qaeda fighters, allowing the ODAs to zero in on their positions, although opinions varied on its accuracy. The teams also carried a number of thermal and night vision optics, including the older AN/PVS-4 night sight and the excellent AN/PAS-13C day/night thermal sight, which could be mounted to the receiver of a rifle or carbine or used as a stand-alone viewer.

All of this equipment had to be carried (along with sufficient ammunition and batteries), by Green Berets and, before wheeled vehicles became available, on the backs of locally procured pack animals. All of an ODA's team and personal equipment was loaded into two packs – one a huge rucksack and the other a smaller daypack that contained both the mission-essential tools and survival necessities that would keep the ODA operational in the field should it lose its main packs. These were known as "bug-out bags" or "go-to-hell packs." Along with their own gear, the ODAs carted in extra weapons and ammunition for the Northern Alliance and extra medical supplies to allow them to establish medical clinics for the locals – a guaranteed way of gaining their trust.

Later in 2001 and into 2002, vehicles would become available including Special Forces modified High Mobility Multipurpose Wheeled Vehicles (HMMWVs) known as the Ground Mobility Vehicle (GMV), Mercedes G-Wagens and standard cargo HMMWVs. A small number of up-armored M1114 HMMWVs also became available in early 2002. All carried mounted .50-cal M2 heavy machine guns and 40mm Mk 19 automatic grenade launchers. The HMMWVs were reliable; however they could not navigate some of the narrow mountain roads of eastern Afghanistan. For this task, the Green Berets also famously used both locally procured Toyota Hilux and US-purchased Toyota Tacoma and Tundra pick-up trucks as well as a number of Land Rover Defenders.

A US Air Force Sikorsky MH-53 Pave Low helicopter as seen through a night vision lens somewhere over Afghanistan. Along with the MH-47s and MH-60s of the 160th Special Operations Aviation Regiment, the MH-53s were instrumental in the early days of the campaign. Sadly the MH-53 flew its final mission, suitably in Afghanistan, in 2008. (AFSOC)

BELIEF AND BELONGING

Special Forces deploying to Afghanistan were united in their common grief stemming from the events of September 11, 2001. Never before had the American homeland suffered such a mass casualty terrorist attack. Even before they were officially placed on a notice to move, the men of the 5th Special Forces Group, with geographic responsibility for Central Asia and thus Afghanistan, were preparing themselves for an imminent

Another iconic image – General Tommy Franks, head of CENTCOM, meeting with an ODA in Afghanistan, October 2001. Note the Mk 12 Mod 0 Special Purpose Rifle and suppressed M4A1 carbine mounting an ACOG sight. (USASOC)

A historic image of Colonel John Mulholland, commander of Task Force Dagger, and the men of several ODAs and ODBs including ODA 555 at the reopening of the American Embassy in Kabul, December 10, 2001. Note the *pakol* flat caps, photographer's vests and *shemaghs*. (USASOC)

deployment.[3] Those on leave or on courses did all they could to return to the home of the 5th Special Forces at Fort Bragg, North Carolina. Nobody wanted to be left behind on what would prove to be the greatest and most successful US Army Special Forces mission of all time.

The respect for the men and women of the NYPD and FDNY who perished in the destruction of the Twin Towers and the raw thirst for revenge for their deaths was evident in the assortment of patches, T-shirts and baseball caps bearing their insignia that the men of the Special Forces wore. Pieces of twisted steel from Ground Zero were even sent to Colonel John Mulholland, the commander of the recently formed Joint Special Operations Task Force-North, better known as Task Force Dagger, so that teams could ceremoniously bury a piece of the Twin Towers on the Afghan battlefield.

The Green Berets who deployed to Afghanistan felt the huge responsibility of being the first US military ground units to respond to the terrorist attacks in New York and Washington. They also felt a tremendous responsibility weighing on them from their forefathers, ranging back to the Jedburghs and the Vietnam-era ODAs. This was a classic Special Forces mission – covertly insert into a hostile nation and conduct Unconventional Warfare and Foreign Internal Defense tasks, all the while with the eyes of the world on them and ever-present political pressure from the White House and Pentagon.

Mulholland's Task Force Dagger was built around his 5th Special Forces Group. The Group comprised three Special Forces Battalions with a headquarters group. Around 1,400 men served in a battalion, with 600 or so in the ODAs themselves. Each battalion was formed of three Special Forces Companies along with a support and headquarters function.[4] These Special Forces Companies were made up of six ODAs and an ODB or Operational Detachment Bravo. The ODB was the command and control element for the Company.

3   There are seven Special Forces Groups today – five regular Army and two National Guard. Each has a geographic responsibility: the 1st the Pacific; the 3rd sub-Saharan Africa; the 5th the Middle East and Central Asia; the 7th Southern and Central Americas; the 10th Europe; the 19th the Pacific and the Middle East; and the 20th Latin America.

4   One company in each Group is assigned as the Commander's In-Extremis Force (CIF), which operates as a Direct Action unit to respond to regional emergencies, including conducting time-sensitive hostage rescues, aircrew recoveries or non-combatant evacuations.

A Green Beret examines a captured Soviet DShK 12.7mm heavy machine gun on an anti-aircraft tripod. His SPEAR BALCS body armor and MOLLE pouches are clearly visible. (JZW)

Each ODA was composed of a 12-man A-Team of two officers – the ODA team or detachment leader (a captain) and his assistant team leader (a chief warrant officer, known as the "Chief"); and ten sergeants. Eight of these sergeants specialized in a Special Forces MOS with two skilled in each MOS – Medical, Weapons, Communications and Engineering. Another senior NCO was assigned the intelligence sergeant role and the final man was appointed as the operations sergeant, better known as the team sergeant, a role not dissimilar to a platoon sergeant in conventional units. Both a junior and a senior sergeant were assigned in each MOS in the ODA to allow roles to be filled should battlefield casualties occur.

As the detachment leader of ODA 595, one of the first Special Forces teams into Afghanistan, commented in a PBS interview:

> This detachment primarily focuses on Unconventional Warfare. In doing that, in training for that type of mission, all the members of the detachment are thoroughly trained in communications, thoroughly cross-trained in communications, basic medical skills, first aid, initial trauma assessment, etc., as well as weapons proficiency of all types.
>
> And that also includes all of us being cross-trained in calling in close air support. This higher degree of cross-training allows us to operate and train in small two-man elements up to 12 men. The team has done this for years. And that is their standard operating procedure.

The officers generally served only two years on an ODA, while the sergeants might have stayed for many years. However, it was not until 1987 that Special Forces had been placed on an even par with other branches of the Army, such as the armor and the cavalry, allowing a Special Forces soldier to stay within the branch rather than having to leave for promotion. The ODAs also had an Air Force Combat Controller (known as a CCT) attached for the duration of their deployment. CCTs were trained to operate alongside special operations forces as ground FACs, guiding in close air support. For their mission in Afghanistan, the CCT would prove essential.

The structure of the ODAs meant that every man felt a strong kinship with his team. In the field, ODAs are expected to be able to operate in sub-units as small as two. Trust in one's fellow soldiers was paramount. The maturity of the Special Forces soldier meant that minor squabbles and personal dislikes between ODA members were shelved for the greater good of the team and the mission. ODAs can become parochial on deployment and are sometimes seen as arrogant by conventional forces. This tends to be the result of working in small, isolated teams that must depend solely on each other to survive. Conventional units that have had longer-term dealings with ODAs inevitably find them to be helpful and generous with their experience and expertise.

ON CAMPAIGN: OPERATION *ENDURING FREEDOM* – AFGHANISTAN

The United States responded surprisingly quickly to the events of September 11, 2001. For many, the assumption was that military SOF would be first into Afghanistan to hunt down Osama bin Laden and al-Qaeda. In fact, the Pentagon was in a state of abject indecision. What became known as "pre 9/11 thinking" dominated – there was no Combat-Search-And-Rescue (CSAR) or reliable aeromedical evacuation system in place to support any SOF ground forces. Additionally there were confusion and arguments over who exactly should be sent, with each service making its own representations in favor of its branch's SOF.

Ultimately, while the Pentagon delayed, the Central Intelligence Agency (CIA) grasped the ball and ran with it. A scratch team of veteran operatives from the Agency's Special Activities Division (SAD) and Counter Terrorism Center (CTC) was to act as the first "pilot" teams into Afghanistan. These Agency teams, operating under the callsign Jawbreaker but formally designated the Northern Alliance Liaison Team (NALT), were assigned a number of pressing tasks – to make initial contact with several of the Afghan warlords who made up the anti-Taliban Northern Alliance; identify and assess targets for the aerial bombing campaign; act as an *in extremis* CSAR capability; and pave the way for the eventual deployment of US Army Special Forces. To help facilitate successful relations with the warlords, the CIA operatives took several million dollars in hard currency with them that ensured compliancy if not loyalty.

The Northern Alliance was a loosely aligned network of warlord-controlled militias which, when they weren't fighting among themselves or switching sides, fought against the Taliban as the only credible opposition in Afghanistan. Their military leader, and the man who kept the warlords in check, Ahmad Shah Massoud, had been assassinated by al-Qaeda on the eve of the terrorist attacks in the United States.

The American plan was to join forces with the Northern Alliance

Why we fight. A USAF special operations MH-53, similar to the type soon to be infiltrating Green Beret teams into Afghanistan, involved in relief operations over central Manhattan and the still-smoking ruins of the World Trade Center. (USAF photograph by Gary Ell)

Afghans, embedding Special Forces teams to act as both mentors and as forward air controllers – giving the guerrilla army its own air support. Initially, the objective was for the Special Forces to enable conventional forces to arrive to prosecute the war alongside the Afghans and topple the Taliban government in an effort that would take an estimated year or more. As the Army Special Operations Forces (ARSOF) official history, *Weapon of Choice* explains: "Around April or May 2002, this new, Special Forces-trained, anti-Taliban army was to begin a spring offensive to secure the northern tier of Afghan cities … Then, perhaps

Special Forces soldiers meet with local Afghan villagers. The central Green Beret's M4A1 is unusual in that it lacks any kind of optical sight or the standard carrying handle. He also wears an aftermarket load-carrying vest. (JZW)

later that year, a general offensive toward Kabul could be launched." Events would soon overtake that thinking, proving even the most optimistic timings wildly incorrect.

The first CIA Jawbreaker team inserted covertly by CIA helicopter into the Panjshir Valley, north of the Afghan capital of Kabul, on the night of September 26, 2001. The operatives, several of whom were former Special Forces soldiers, met with the Afghan warlord Fahim Khan, Massoud's successor as military commander of the Northern Alliance. Meanwhile, four ODAs from the 5th Special Forces Group had been ordered into pre-mission isolation in ISOFACs (Isolation Facility) at Fort Bragg, developing their operational plans while awaiting forward deployment to a former Russian airbase in Uzbekistan called Karshi-Khanabad (K2). K2 would provide the initial launch site for the ODAs to strike into Afghanistan.

There was some natural disquiet at rumors that the CIA had been "first in", but the ODAs were eager to ensure they wouldn't be "bumped" from the operation. At Fort Bragg, supplementary and non-standard equipment was purchased with their government-issue credit cards, such as civilian cold-weather gear, GPS units and Camelbak hydration packs, along with most of the town's supplies of batteries. For those lucky teams already in the ISOFACs, they ordered and pawed over copies of Lester Grau's pioneering tactical study of the Soviet–Afghan War, *The Bear Went over the Mountain*. Finally, Colonel John Mulholland, commander of the 5th Special Forces Group and now commander of Task Force Dagger, gathered the men together in their Team Room and said the words the ODAs had been waiting to hear: "Gentlemen, you have been selected to infiltrate Afghanistan."

The plan was simple if dramatic. With the anti-Taliban Northern Alliance already in contact with the advance CIA NALT teams, it made sense to infiltrate into the north with the ODAs and begin the war from there. The north of the country was also readily accessible from K2 and from Pakistan (where the early CSAR contingency teams would be based, along with a Ranger Quick Reaction Force).

Other options were considered, including training an Afghan guerrilla army in a neighboring country, which was decided against as it would take too long

A combat controller uses an AN/PEQ-1 Special Operations Forces Laser Acquisition Marker (SOFLAM) to mark a target for a laser-guided bomb. Note the wrist compass worn on his right hand. (USASOC)

to do; or concurrently inserting ODAs into the south – this was scratched as there were no organized anti-Taliban forces in the southern provinces, nor were any CIA advance teams in place.

The Special Forces teams would infiltrate into northern Afghanistan in October, mentor and partner with the Northern Alliance over the winter months with the objective of launching the ground offensive supported by American and British airpower in the spring. Events would quickly overtake these plans. Historically, the Special Forces had been a subordinate command supporting conventional forces in what the military termed "the main effort." Now the roles were reversed and the Green Berets became the main effort while the rest of the US military supported them. ODAs from the 3rd Battalion, 5th Special Forces Group were the first Army Special Forces on the ground in Afghanistan and became the tip of the spear.[5]

The ODAs would initially link up with two anti-Taliban leaders, Mohammed Fahim Khan, who had succeeded Ahmad Shah Massoud as the Northern Alliance's military commander, and General Rashid Dostum, an Uzbek warlord who led the largest militia army in northern Afghanistan. Dostum, like many of the Afghan warlords, had a checkered history. He had been in the Soviet Army before joining the communist Democratic Republic of Afghanistan (DRA) government during the Soviet–Afghan War. He later joined the mujahideen insurgency, fighting against his former masters. During the Afghan Civil War of the 1990s, he briefly fought with the Taliban before siding with the Northern Alliance. Such swirling loyalties were not uncommon.

5   In early October, a second Joint Special Operations Task Force, known as Task Force K-Bar after the Marine fighting knife, was stood up under Navy SEAL Captain Robert Harward. K-Bar comprised SEAL Teams 2, 3 and 8 and the Green Berets of the 1st Battalion of the 3rd Special Forces Group along with what would become the largest international SOF contingent. A third task force later known as Sword or Task Force 11 was also established from Joint Special Operations Command (JSOC) special mission units.

 REAL-WORLD COIN – PARTNERING WITH THE NORTHERN ALLIANCE

This image is an amalgamation of several roles the Special Forces undertook in Afghanistan. In the background, a Green Beret can be seen tutoring an Afghan militiaman in basic marksmanship principles with his AK47 rifle. In the middle ground, an attached Air Force Combat Controller is marking a target with his AN/PEQ-1 Special Operations Forces Laser Acquisition Marker or SOFLAM that "paints" a target with an invisible laser beam, allowing laser-guided smart-bombs such as the Paveway series to home in on the beam (high above rumbles a B-1B Lancer strategic bomber conducting close air support). Finally, in the foreground is a Special Forces detachment leader developing a concept of operations with an Afghan G-Chief (any resemblance to a certain Uzbek general is purely coincidental).

Note that the Green Berets and the combat controller are attired in typical 2001 fashion – desert pattern DCUs, civilian shirts, Afghan *pakols* and American baseball caps, and the ubiquitous beard and Oakley sunglasses. All are armed with the 9mm Beretta M9 sidearm or the 5.56mm M4A1 carbine.

One of the many tasks of a Special Forces 18 Bravo Engineering Sergeant – the safe demolition of unexploded ordnance (UXO) on the battlefield including a dud Taliban mortar and artillery rounds. (JZW)

Infiltration: October 2001

For the purposes of our narrative, we will illustrate the Special Forces involvement in the early phases of Operation *Enduring Freedom* by using a fictional ODA. Our fictional ODA, drawn from the 5th Special Forces Group (Airborne), will operate under the fictional callsign of Copperhead Zero One. We will pick up its story in mid-October 2001, at K2 in Uzbekistan where the team has forward deployed to flooded tents and mud as the winter weather began to move in. Alongside Copperhead Zero One are a number of other 5th Group ODAs – the first slated to insert into Afghanistan once the weather permitted was ODA 555 (known as the Triple Nickel) and ODA 595.

The night of October 7 saw Operation *Crescent Wind* begin with airstrikes by land-based strategic bombers, carrier-based F/A-18 Hornets and more than 50 Tomahawk TLAM (Tomahawk Land Attack Missile) cruise missiles launched from US Navy and Royal Navy ships and submarines. These repeatedly pounded Taliban and al-Qaeda targets in Afghanistan, leading to then Secretary of Defense, Donald Rumsfeld to quip at a press briefing that "we're not running out of targets … Afghanistan is." By October 10, CENTCOM declared total air domination. On the 13th, the ODAs received their final orders to "initiate the UW campaign in Afghanistan." If only the weather would clear, the ODAs could insert and begin that mission.

While they waited, the ODAs conducted equipment and weapons checks and carried out any preventive maintenance they could. Next of kin or death letters were written and secreted in the event tragedy should occur, and the teams packed and repacked, weighing the importance of every piece of equipment. Alongside the Special Forces men were the aviators of both the

A Green Beret zeroes his camouflage-painted M4A1 carbine using the attached ACOG optic. He wears the SPEAR BALCS body armor and pouches, DCU trousers and a civilian hunting cap. (JZW)

Army's 160th Special Operations Aviation Regiment (SOAR or more commonly known as the Nightstalkers) and the Air Force's 20th Special Operations Squadron. The 160th SOAR had the mission to ferry the ODAs into Afghanistan in their MH-47E Chinook and MH-60L Blackhawks while the Air Force had the primary CSAR responsibility (although Air Force MH-53E Pave Low helicopters would themselves also later insert a number of ODAs).

On the night and early morning of October 18–19, word spread throughout K2 that the first two teams – ODAs 555 and 595 – had been successfully inserted into Northern Afghanistan by Army MH-47Es. During the same night cycle, the Rangers had also conducted an airfield seizure outside Kandahar while a Delta Force squadron raided Mullah Omar's nearby compound. Only the Delta raid encountered any resistance. The Special Forces were finally on the ground.

Copperhead Zero One's chance would soon come. On the night of October 21, the men climbed into an MH-47E, dragging packs weighing an easy 100 pounds. They wore a mix of American three-color desert BDUs and high-end civilian outdoor clothing under Afghan shawls to protect against the still terrible weather. Most tucked Afghan *pakol* hats or baseball caps into pockets as they fitted bulky AN/PVS-18 night vision goggles over their heads and ensured they had fitted infrared reflective glint tape to their gear to allow them to be recognized as friendly forces through night vision devices. The cabin lights in the MH-47E were red filtered to maintain their night vision. After what seemed like an exasperating wait on the tarmac, the Nightstalker crew chief gave the thumbs up and, accompanied by a pair of escorting MH-60L Direct Action Penetrators (DAPs – armed gunship versions of the Blackhawk), the Chinook lifted off into the night sky.

The weather was still a danger to the aircraft, and as the flight neared the 16,000-foot peaks of the Hindu Kush mountain range bordering Afghanistan, the DAPs were forced to turn back, leaving the Chinook to fly on alone. Dust storms from the desert plains beyond the mountains reduced visibility, even at 10,000 feet, to less than half a mile. Coupled with the very real chance of fatal ice build-ups on their rotor blades, the helicopters experienced some of the worst flying conditions on the planet. Incredibly, the Chinook still arrived at

FRONT

UP TO $25,000,000 REWARD

AIMAN AL-ZAWAHIRI   USAMA BIN LADEN

BACK

PUSHTO		DARI
UP TO A $25,000,000 REWARD FOR INFORMATION LEADING TO THE WHEREABOUTS OR CAPTURE OF THESE TWO MEN.	 USAMA BIN LADEN / AIMAN AL-ZAWAHIRI	UP TO A $25,000,000 REWARD FOR INFORMATION LEADING TO THE WHEREABOUTS OR CAPTURE OF THESE TWO MEN.

The English-language version of a PSYOPS leaflet dropped in its thousands over Afghanistan offering huge rewards for information leading to the capture of al-Qaeda high-value targets. (USASOC)

the designated landing zone in Afghanistan within the prescribed time on target, plus or minus 30 seconds as promised by the Nightstalkers.[6]

Looking out from the Chinook, the ODA could see armed men ringing the Landing Zone (LZ) – the Nightstalker crew chief remarked that they looked like "Sand People" from *Star Wars*. CIA operatives from the NALT, along with a locally recruited Afghan militia, were there to meet them with infrared strobes to mark the LZ. The Chinook touched down briefly, the ODA ran off the ramp into the darkness and, following doctrine, established 360-degree security around the aircraft before it lifted off for the long and dangerous flight back to K2. Copperhead Zero One was met by a former Navy SEAL CIA operative named "Phil" who made brief introductions to an Afghan militia fighter, who was evidently the warlord's number-two man, before ushering the team into a number of Toyota Hilux trucks to begin the next stage of its journey.

At a local village, the team leader was taken to an audience with the warlord by the CIA operative. The Green Beret, a captain in the Army rank structure, was introduced as a colonel, as higher ranks impress Afghans, including the warlords of the Northern Alliance who routinely called themselves generals (Afghan warlords would often refer to ODA members as "commanders"). An agreement was reached to meet in the morning to begin planning. The ODA then spent an uneasy first night in the warlord's village, keeping one eye open and its weapons to hand. Its intelligence was still sadly lacking on many of the Afghans it would be working with, and in martial Afghan society, swapping sides was not considered particularly duplicitous.

The following morning, the warlord was nowhere to be found and, according to the CIA liaison, had important business elsewhere with a relative. The ODA would soon learn that the Afghans worked to their own schedules, and tribal and family responsibilities trumped even overthrowing the Taliban. The warlord returned later that day and the ODA team leader and the CIA man sat down to many cups of hot sweet chai (tea). The Green Beret was quizzed in detail by the warlord about his and his team's intentions before finally discussing how the ODA could help. The warlord had yet to see American airpower in action, although he had heard of the "American death ray" from his cousins. He was anxious to see it in practice for himself and arrangements were made to travel to the front line the following day.

Before then, the ODA established itself in several compound buildings in the village, which would serve as its base for the immediate future. Sandbags,

---

6 Amazingly, this actually occurred to the second ODA into Afghanistan – ODA 595 on the night of October 19. The official history states that the pilots were forced to "push their helicopters to the limits of aircraft design performance." Both of their escorting DAPs were forced to return to K2 because of the adverse weather conditions. An ODA detachment commander explained: "we hit a surprise sand storm and heavy fog which created near-zero visibility conditions, and the armed escort aircraft had to turn back, and we flew alone through the mountains the remainder of that trip. And the pilot gave us a perfect infiltration."

building materials and HESCO barriers (collapsible earth-filled fortifications) were added to the list for the first resupply. As it stood, if he got past the warlord's less than dutiful sentries, any insurgent could walk into the village and lob a grenade into the Americans' quarters. The ODA posted its own watch just in case.

Food was initially restricted to Meals Ready to Eat (MREs) until the team was formally invited to break bread with the Afghans. Although the ODAs had received extensive vaccinations, the Special Forces Medics carried with them copious amounts of Cipro and other broad-based antibiotics to combat local bugs, which could be picked up from Afghan cooking practices. Because of the malaria risk in certain areas, the soldiers had already started a course of Mefloquine, an anti-malarial drug known to cause disturbed sleep and in extreme cases hallucinations – for that reason, several of the ODA had decided against taking it and took their chances.

The following morning, one of the warlord's lieutenants arrived with a group of horseback-mounted militia fighters (dubbed Afghan Militia Fighters or AMF) and a collection of Afghan horses in tow for the Americans to ride. There were several challenges that were immediately obvious to the ODA. Firstly, the Afghan Lokai horses were more like ponies in stature to the taller Westerners. Secondly, they were all stallions and constantly fought among themselves, making them not the easiest introduction to riding. Thirdly, the traditional Afghan saddle was made from wood and was incredibly uncomfortable for those not accustomed to it, which was all of the ODA.

A Special Forces operator with an EO Tech Holographic Weapons Sight equipped M4A1. Behind him is a cargo HMMWV modified into a field expedient GMV with seating in the tray bed. (JZW)

The horses also proved a tactical challenge for the ODAs – the detachment leader of ODA 595 told his men, "keep your feet light in the stirrups. If anyone is thrown by his mount and has a foot in the stirrup and the horse doesn't stop immediately, the nearest man has to shoot the horse dead." The stirrups were designed for Afghans who do not wear American-sized combat boots and were dangerously tight. If a man was thrown on a mountain trail, he would be seriously injured or even killed if the horse bolted. The ODAs requested, and received several weeks later, lightweight Australian Cordura saddles, better suited to Westerners and the diminutive size of the Afghan stallions (although by this time they had largely transitioned to locally procured Toyotas that were somewhat less temperamental than the steeds).

The Captain of ODA 595 later commented on the experience, "All these guys [the ODAs] did an incredibly magnificent job learning how to ride under those type of conditions, the first time in combat. A few of them had ridden horses when they were five or six years old ... and now they're learning how to ride in combat in mountainous terrain, narrow treacherous mountain cliffs, often riding at night. And there are mines in the area. Over the next several weeks, we were riding 10–30 kilometers [6–20 miles] per day."

Before the ODA took charge of its new transport, the warlord arrived with another band of militiamen and called an immediate meeting. He sat with his key lieutenant, the detachment commander, and the ODA's Warrant Officer

Members of ODA 595 come to grips with their local transport. Close examination reveals that the Green Berets in this image have not yet received their resupply of Cordura Western-style saddles and are using Afghan wooden saddles. (USASOC)

while chai was served. A map was spread on the carpets and the Afghan began to point out nearby Taliban positions. This was where he wanted the American bombs to strike. The Green Berets agreed and marked the targets on their own maps to pass to their attached Air Force Combat Controller who would coordinate the airstrikes. The plan was simple – the ODA would split with a half-team, including the Combat Controller, accompanying the warlord to the front line. The other half-team would stay at the village and establish the compound as a headquarters.

As quickly as the meeting had begun, it ended, and the warlord and his men mounted up. The ODA, few with any riding experience, cautiously climbed aboard the Afghan horses provided. Their packs and the mission-essential SOFLAM laser designator were loaded upon tethered donkeys. They rode for several hours before stopping at a low rise overlooking a desert plain where the warlord pointed out the enemy positions. Through binoculars, the ODA could see Taliban moving around several buildings in the distance. Parked nearby were several Toyota trucks and an ageing BTR-60 armored personnel carrier. The Combat Controller saw this as a perfect opportunity to demonstrate the SOFLAM.

While the SOFLAM was powered up and affixed to its tripod, the Combat Controller spoke to an orbiting AWACS (Airborne-Warning-And-Control-System: a command and control aircraft that acted as an intermediary between the ground controller and the fighter-bombers) that vectored two Navy F-14 Tomcat jet fighters carrying a number of GBU-16 1,000-pound laser-guided bombs toward the ODA's location. The Combat Controller used the SOFLAM to "lase" the BTR-60 and awaited the arrival of the Tomcats. The pair of jets soon appeared overhead and the Combat Controller went to work on his radio, confirming their target, the location of friendly forces and the safest and most effective angle of attack. Finally he beckoned the detachment leader forward and gave him a warning that the bomb was inbound. The Afghan

THE ANCIENT AND LESS THAN NOBLE ART OF BUZKASHI

The typical Afghan stallion and his Green Beret rider – now mythologized in Special Forces history as the "Horse Soldiers" – join a game of *buzkashi*. The horses were primarily a mountain breed known as the Lokai, originally bred by Uzbek tribesmen as both packhorses and riding horses and were closer to ponies in stature to the Americans. The Lokai were used in the most popular sport in Afghanistan, and one which several Green Berets participated in, *buzkashi*. *Buzkashi* ("goat bashing") has been compared to a cross between polo, rugby and hockey – all while mounted. Players attempt to drag a beheaded goat across a marked line. Perhaps not surprisingly, its practice was banned by the Taliban.

The Afghan saddles also proved problematic, being made of wood and with stirrups that were far too small for combat boot-clad feet (the saddle used for the basis of this illustration is a saddle of the period held by the CIA at their CIA Museum at Langley). Nevertheless, the ODAs rode these horses into battle alongside their Northern Alliance allies, with new, Western-style saddles arriving only after several weeks of operation, by which time the ODAs had procured Toyota pick-up trucks to replace their horses.

A Special Forces soldier scans the horizon with his M4A1/ M203 while an Afghan militiaman uses a locally procured radio set, apparently powered by a car battery. Note the satellite antennae array at the feet of the Green Beret and the fact that he still wears his NBC respirator bag on his left thigh in case of chemical attack, a genuine fear as the US faced al-Qaeda on the battlefield for the first time. (USASOC)

warlord was invited to watch through the SOFLAM's sight.

According to an ODA member later interviewed on PBS, "Due to the altitude that the aircraft was flying with the laser-guided munitions, when it dropped its ordnance the bomb was falling for a minute and half to two minutes. If you timed it just right, as the laser target designator is engaging [the] enemy position, you let your Northern Alliance commander take a look through the laser target designator. He sees it going, but he doesn't see the bombs fly into the target. He hears that chirping noise from the laser target designator and then the enemy position explodes. They believe that we have the death ray, and this was a myth that we were willing to perpetuate."[7]

Moments later the BTR, the parked technicals, and the Taliban fighters all disappeared in a massive explosion and dust cloud that briefly seemed to shadow the sun. The warlord was impressed. He clapped the Special Forces men on the back and with a wide grin declared that with this "death ray" the Taliban would not stand a chance. He immediately used his Motorola handheld radio to call up the nearby Taliban and inform them that the Americans had arrived and now they were all doomed. That evening, the warlord treated the ODA as honored guests with a huge banquet meal before presenting the detachment commander with a list of targets for the next day.

This was the Green Berets' first exposure to local cuisine. The Afghans ate communally with everyone seated on carpets and rugs on the floor. The food was served on large shared plates and normally comprised at least one type of meat – chicken or lamb was common – fresh salad often incorporating tomatoes, rice, flatbread and a range of pickled fruits and vegetables. Diners scoop the food up with their right hand as the left hand is considered unclean in Islamic cultures. The food is washed down with *shlombeh* (a yogurt-based drink), chai or soft drinks.

Northern Afghanistan resupply – by horse and donkey. The ODAs had to adapt quickly to the ways of war from another era. Eventually World War II-issue field manuals on operating with pack animals were airdropped to the teams. (USASOC)

After the meal, the team reflected on its first day of taking the war to the Taliban. Morale was still exceedingly high after the terrorist attacks in New York and Washington and the ODAs felt they were contributing to the national healing. There was also the feeling that Afghanistan was the first opportunity since Vietnam to really prove Special Forces' worth in their core skill of Unconventional Warfare to topple the Taliban regime. The ODAs were nevertheless keen to go after any al-Qaeda targets that presented themselves, as they knew that ultimately this was their primary mission. Until sufficient numbers of Delta Force

7 This myth of the ODAs possessing death rays and similar was only enhanced by the deployment of an AC-130 Spectre fixed-wing gunship with a female weapons officer who Northern Alliance General Dostum convinced the Taliban fighters was an angel of death in the heavens, and that she was working for him. Once the Taliban heard the female voice and the Spectre firing from the night sky, they were convinced and many soon surrendered.

operators infiltrated into the country and Task Force Sword was stood up to hunt al-Qaeda, the ODAs were responsible for Direct Action missions against any identified high-value targets.

Working with the Afghans was proving a unique experience. The ODAs fell back on their theater-specific training, their Robin Sage experiences and Lawrence of Arabia's *Twenty Seven Articles* that, although written in 1917 with Arabs in mind, was equally applicable to working with Afghans in 2001: "Better [they] do it tolerably than that you do it perfectly. It is their war, and you are to help them, not to win it for them." The ODAs were there to mentor and guide the Afghans, not to fight the war themselves. In Western terms, the Afghans were enthusiastic but displayed little understanding of small-unit tactics – they and their opponents fought in a particularly Afghan way.

The Afghan way of war was certainly alien to the Special Forces men. The AMF would make a pretense of firing a lot of rounds in the enemy's general direction before retiring, content that their duty had been completed. Curiously, it was commonplace for the Northern Alliance to talk with the Taliban via cheap, commercial radios, both to admonish their opponents with crude taunts and to offer surrender terms.[8] Many battles would be decided through negotiation after the face-saving but ineffective combat phase was completed. The Afghans were far from professional soldiers despite long experience in irregular warfare. The archetype of the mujahideen marksman also proved largely a myth – with endemic eye health issues and poor weapons maintenance, the Afghans were less than average shots on the whole.

The Afghans were also very concerned that even one American death would cause the Americans to leave – General Dostum is quoted as having said, "five hundred of my men can be killed but not one American can even be injured or you will leave." (Dostum at one point did not allow the Americans to come any closer than 5 miles from the Taliban, forcing them to use map coordinate estimates to guide in aerial bombs with a resulting loss of accuracy.) Apparently, the Afghans had seen the US response to the Battle of the Black Sea in Somalia a decade earlier and feared a similar outcome should the "Ameriki" begin taking casualties. They had not reckoned on the depth of national feeling both back in the United States and among the Special Forces teams deploying to Afghanistan. The ODAs saw themselves as the terrible, swift sword of the American people, an instrument of both justice and revenge against al-Qaeda and their allies the Taliban.

Winning hearts and minds – a Special Forces 18 Delta Medical Sergeant holds a walk-in clinic for Afghan civilians. Although he has stripped off his body armor, he keeps a holstered 9mm Beretta M9 handy. (USASOC)

8   These radios were also used to trick the Taliban into conducting bomb damage assessments of airstrikes. The Northern Alliance soldiers would impersonate Taliban on the radios that all used an unsecured common frequency and ask whether the bombs had done any damage. Their replies allowed the combat controllers to adjust the drop of the next bomb. According to one ODA member, "… that guy who was basically saying how far we missed them by would no longer be there. You'd hear people on the other end of the radio complaining or upset about a friend he'd lost on the radio."

ODA members and their AMF atop a Northern Alliance T-55 main battle tank, a relic from the Afghan Civil War. Note the Northern Alliance crest painted as an insignia and recently issued American woodland BDUs worn by the AMF to attempt to counter friendly fire. (JZW)

USAF Combat Controller Staff Sergeant Bart Decker attached to ODA 595 astride an Afghan pony. (USASOC)

At the time, according to Eric Blehm's excellent *The Only Thing Worth Dying For*, there were only "thirty-six Green Berets in-country, close to sixty ready to infiltrate from K2, and a handful of Delta Force teams." These hundred or so Special Forces and their colleagues in the CIA and Delta would soon have an effect radically disproportionate to their numbers.

Turning the tide: November to December 2001

Copperhead Zero One began to "service" each target on the warlord's list. The targets would be cleared with CENTCOM and the CIA before being passed to the detachment leadership and the Combat Controller to assign priorities. With only one SOFLAM designator and one Combat Controller, the ODA felt it was restricted in the number of targets it could hit each day. Some of the Green Berets were qualified Ground Forward Air Controllers (G-FACs) and could guide in airstrikes, but the lack of additional radios and SOFLAM units precluded this. A resupply eventually brought in an additional SOFLAM and two extra radios, only one of which the communications sergeant could actually get to work, a common occurrence in the dusty Afghan environment.

This enabled the ODA to do what it had trained for and split down into three four-man sub-teams. One remained at the village to maintain the headquarters and act as an ad-hoc Quick Reaction Force; one travelled with the warlord's party heading toward the local Taliban-controlled population center; and one set off with the Combat Controller to destroy an entrenched Taliban position to the east. Across the country, other ODAs were following similar orders – splitting down into sub-teams of mixed Green Berets and CIA operatives. (Doctrinally, when an ODA splits in two, the sub-teams are known as the Alpha and Bravo teams.) As the weather fortuitously cleared over the Hindu Kush, further ODAs began infiltrating into Afghanistan every few days. Owing to the excellent situation reports filed by the early teams, these ODAs arrived far better prepared in terms of both equipment and understanding of the local situation.

Other non-Special Forces units were also arriving – the Ranger Reconnaissance Detachment had conducted a HALO jump to secure a remote landing strip for a Delta Force squadron, which arrived with its specially adapted Pinzgauer trucks. The units conducted a range of mounted reconnaissance and Direct Action missions ambushing Taliban convoys. Another Delta team developed a plan to rescue several NGO workers captured by the Taliban by posing as al-Qaeda fighters, but the hostages were released safely through negotiation.

The ODAs continued to work alongside the Afghan militias and their warlord leaders, mentoring and guiding. When the opportunity presented itself, the ODAs taught classes to the AMF in basic marksmanship, tactics, and field first aid. As many of the warlords were former enemies brought together principally only by

The accoutrements of modern war – a tripod-mounted Soviet DShK heavy machine gun, a satellite antennae array, an AN/PRC-137 high-frequency radio, a SOFLAM laser marker and an Mk 12 Special Purpose Rifle. (USASOC)

CIA dollars, the ODAs had to de-conflict the warlords themselves. The detachment leaders – one-part diplomat, one-part military adviser – were a constant presence at their warlord's side, continuously refining their battle plans as the power of American airstrikes became apparent to the Afghan G-Chiefs. Slowly but surely, they began to see results.

It began with ODAs 534 and 595. On November 10, Mazar-e-Sharif, Afghanistan's second-largest city and a key objective in the north, fell to the Northern Alliance. It had been defended by the feared al-Qaeda Brigade 55 which nevertheless quickly melted away as General Dostum's forces advanced under American air cover. It would prove an archetype for the fall of other key cities – a mixture of intimidation, negotiation, and aerial firepower. As an ODA sergeant mentioned in a PBS interview, "... something that's key in all this is that both Northern Alliance and enemy communications were, for the most part, CB radios. They would be arguing with each other in the heat of battle. The Taliban would be saying, 'Nanny, nanny, boo, boo' and the Northern Alliance would be saying, 'Hey, we're coming to get you.'"

The ODAs had to ensure that any prisoners taken were humanely treated – the Afghans had no knowledge of the Rules of Land Warfare or the Geneva Conventions and often treated prisoners, particularly foreign fighters, brutally. Additionally, the ODAs had to operate as warrior-diplomats to intercede between rival warlord factions – many of the warlords had fought at various times for the former Communist government in Kabul, the Taliban and the Northern Alliance and were often bitter enemies.

While our fictional Copperhead Zero One and its real-life counterparts were orchestrating the collapse of Taliban resistance in the north, events were proceeding at a heady pace in the south. ODA 574 was tasked to infiltrate into the south, "link up with Hamid Karzai and his Pashtun fighters, and advise and assist his forces to destabilize and eliminate the Taliban regime." Before joining up with ODA 574, Karzai had spent a month in Afghanistan attempting to drum up support for an anti-Taliban militia. He was eventually pursued by the Taliban and nearly killed before he was rescued on November 3 in Uruzgan Province by a US Navy SEAL element. Linking up with future Afghan President Karzai and his militia in Uruzgan, it became readily apparent to ODA 574 that the provincial capital – Tarin Kowt – was vital to capturing the south.

Taliban leader Mullah Omar lived nearby and the area, along with neighboring Kandahar, was considered the spiritual home of the Taliban movement. Matters were taken out of their hands when the residents of Tarin Kowt rose up against the Taliban at Karzai's urging. ODA 574 was forced to deploy into the city, taking up defensive positions overlooking the strategic

A Special Forces soldier flanked by two Civil Affairs soldiers escort a Taliban detainee to an EPW enclosure. (JZW)

road from Kandahar, to guard against Taliban reinforcements.

They did not have to wait long. Soon long columns of Taliban vehicles were approaching. The Combat Controller went to work and Air Force and Navy strike aircraft began targeting the convoy. Karzai's militia panicked at the close proximity of the Taliban and fled, forcing the ODA to follow. After Karzai's personal intervention with his militia, a second defensive position was occupied and the Taliban reinforcements were destroyed piecemeal with over 300 killed.

After the capture of Mazar-e-Sharif, Tarin Kowt, and soon after Herat and Bagram, the dominoes began to fall. On November 13, the Afghan capital of Kabul fell to the warlord Fahim Khan. The men of the Triple Nickel, ODA 555, entered the city on only their 26th day in Afghanistan, far less than the year that many strategists had expected. According to reports from the team, they and Fahim Khan's men were met as liberators by chanting crowds.

ODA 583 was inserted into the south from Pakistan by MH-53 helicopters to link up with Gul Agha Sherzai, and by late November was also closing on Kandahar. As the birthplace of the Taliban, Kandahar was seen as even more strategically important than the capital, Kabul. If Kandahar fell, then the country fell to the Northern Alliance. The Taliban, not surprisingly, fought a ferocious defense, with ODA 583's three sub-units (each equipped with a Combat Controller and a SOFLAM) working 24-hour shifts calling in airstrikes around Kandahar Airport. Karzai's forces massed for a final attack on the city in a mounted convoy that one Green Beret officer described as a cross between "off-road races and scenes from the movie *Mad Max*."

Until this point in the war, the men of the Special Forces had killed only remotely by guiding in aerial firepower on distant enemies. With the advance on Kandahar, that would change. ODA 574 was involved in a vicious firefight near the Arghendab Bridge on the road to Kandahar. A four-man Special Forces sub-unit killed a number of Taliban with accurate fire from their M4A1 carbines as the majority of the AMF retreated under enemy fire. The sub-unit and 30 AMF held one side of the bridge against a Taliban

 KNOCK, KNOCK – DIRECT ACTION!

ODAs were also called upon to conduct Direct Action missions, targeting high-value individuals within the Taliban and al-Qaeda remnants. These missions were closer to the classic commando mission of popular imagination, with teams surrounding and conducting forced entries on enemy compounds, aiming to capture or kill the targeted individual. Although this helped reduce enemy command and control capabilities as key leaders and facilitators were removed, it also led to accusations of fraud committed by Afghan informants who often informed on business or tribal rivals, denouncing them as insurgents.

This illustration portrays our fictional ODA, callsign Copperhead Zero One, conducting a dynamic entry on a Taliban compound, catching the unfortunate high-value target unawares. Both operators carry the M4A1 SOPMOD carbine mounted with Trijicon ACOG optics. Note that the operators have stripped down to tee shirts or bare sleeves under their BALCS SPEAR amour and Chi-Com chest rigs as the weather becomes warmer..

Members of the 5th Special Forces headquarters staff, including Lieutenant-Colonel Max Bowers at the rear, ride with Uzbek warlord General Abdur Rashid Dostum and ODA 595. (USASOC)

counter-attack of some 100 fighters, calling in Danger Close (within range of hitting friendly forces) supporting fires from a lumbering AC-130 Spectre overhead to break the attack.

Later the next day, the Green Berets were again involved in a firefight at the bridge resulting in one American receiving a gunshot wound. Arghendab Bridge was the first time that any Green Berets had been involved in face-to-face combat with the enemy (which according to signals intercepts, included at least some al-Qaeda fighters speaking Arabic). Soon after, on December 5, ODA 574 was also involved in tragedy when an errant GPS-guided JDAM (Joint Direct Attack Munition) landed among its position, killing three Special Forces soldiers and gravely wounding several more. Approximately 50 AMF were also killed and even Hamid Karzai was lightly wounded.

Those Green Berets with lesser wounds immediately went to work on their colleagues using their Combat Lifesaver training. Soon after, a mounted Delta Force element arrived and the Delta medics joined in the effort. Navy CH-53 helicopters flew in to evacuate wounded as Marine CH-53s brought in ODB 570 and ODA 524, along with medical teams and Air Force Para Rescue Jumpers. Several versions of what went wrong have been advanced, with the most common being the PLGR GPS unit recalibrated to its own position when its batteries were changed. The real reason appears to be that the GPS device could be set on "hasty" or "deliberate" mode with the latter being designed for use with close air support and incorporating an error message if the coordinates were too close to the operator's location. On "hasty" mode, this error message was easily bypassed, which is what may have happened.

Eventually AMF from both Karzai's and Sherzai's competing militias entered Kandahar on December 8, with their attached ODAs desperately attempting to dissuade them from descending into open combat with their rivals. The ODAs could see all of their hard work disappearing into civil war between their Afghan G-Chiefs. Thankfully, this did not occur. Equally worrying was the number of former Taliban who had immediately switched sides to the Northern Alliance – one ODA officer commented, "one minute you're shooting at them, and the next minute they're your allies and friends." No matter, Kandahar had fallen and the Taliban was in tatters, its al-Qaeda allies trying to escape to Pakistan. The first phase of the Afghan campaign was over, and all in a remarkable 49 days of combat operations.

As researcher Linda Robinson points out in her modern history of the Special Forces, *Masters of Chaos*, "No one had ever imagined that fewer than one hundred Special Forces soldiers and an indigenous militia could overthrow a government so quickly."

The US had suffered their first casualties in the fratricide of ODA 574 and the death of a CIA operative, Mike Spann, at the November 25 revolt of Taliban and al-Qaeda prisoners at the so-called "House of War", an ancient fortification near Mazar-e-Sharif, which General Dostum was now using as his headquarters. A Special Forces Operational Detachment Charlie (ODC) team, which responded to the revolt along with a small British Special Boat Service (SBS) element, suffered wounds from another errant JDAM while guiding in strikes to quell the uprising.

A Green Beret from the 3rd Special Forces Group maintains security outside a reinforced Taliban cave entrance during SSE operations. (USASOC)

On December 10, Colonel John Mulholland and the men of ODAs 550, 575 and 555 held a ceremony at the US Embassy in Kabul with the Stars and Stripes flying for the first time in 12 years to commemorate the Special Forces fallen. After a moment of solemn silence, the flag was taken down to allow the Marines to raise it in the official reopening on December 17. Days later, Hamid Karzai was formally named as the transitional leader of a new Afghan Interim Authority (AIA) on December 22, 2001.

Members of an ODA operating in Northern Afghanistan, October 2001. Note the SOFLAM laser designator deployed on its tripod. (USASOC)

The Special Forces men began to spread out and establish safe houses in regional centers such as Khowst and Jalalabad. These safe houses (often termed fire bases in honor of their Green Beret forefathers in Vietnam) would be manned by an ODA, some attached Rangers as force protection, a Civil Affairs team, a smattering of CIA and other intelligence types, perhaps a PSYOP (Psychological Operations) detachment, and a locally recruited Afghan security force. By this point, the Green Beret mission incorporated both Unconventional Warfare and Foreign Internal Defense roles as they trained fledgling Afghan forces, conducted medical clinics and civil improvement programs and conducted offensive operations against Taliban remnants.

Our fictional ODA, Copperhead Zero One, would establish a local safe house in the northeast and raise a force of "strikers" from the local Afghan male population – some of whom were undoubtedly former Taliban but all now keen to work for the Americans and the new government, at least while they were being fed, paid, and equipped by the ODA. These "strikers" or "indigs" (from the Vietnam-era term for indigenous forces) provided both a security and strike force and a built-in local intelligence network.

The ODAs also conducted Direct Action missions, often at the behest of the CIA, with operations mounted by ODAs reinforced with squads of Rangers. These were aimed at al-Qaeda targets, although at this stage of the war, intelligence was poor. This situation was taken advantage of by the warlords and local tribal elders, who passed deliberately false information to the ODAs in the hope that the Green Berets would target their rivals as "Taliban." Unfortunately this did occur as did cases of mistakenly targeting militias that had joined the new government. One Green Beret DA mission in January 2002 ended in a reported 16 enemy dead. It emerged only later that the group of former enemy fighters had apparently switched allegiance to the new transitional government.

Uzbek warlord General Dostum, the team leader of ODA 595 and Dostum's advisers plan his offensive against Mazar-e-Sharif. (USASOC)

This mission involved an SSE (sensitive site exploitation – often a raid followed by a detailed search of a location) on a pair of suspected al-Qaeda compounds in Uruzgan. Three 5th Group ODAs would hit the western compound, code-named Objective Kelly while two further ODAs would strike the eastern compound known as Objective Brigid. A squadron from the New Zealand SAS was on standby to act as a QRF. The raid on Kelly was largely uneventful with only two enemy engaging the Green Berets before they were both

An MH-47 of the 160th SOAR conducts a mid-air refuelling from an MC-130 Combat Talon. (USAF photograph by Technical Sergeant Aaron Cram)

killed. At Brigid, the ODAs ran into concerted opposition. Fierce close-quarter firefights erupted within the compound and a pair of GMVs had to be brought forward to silence one enemy position with 40mm and .50-cal fire. Once the objective was cleared and secured, a flag of the transitional AIA was found during the SSE. It appeared that regrettably the intelligence on the target sites was several weeks old and out of date – the occupants of the target sites, unbeknown to the Special Forces, had changed sides.

The Americans knew little of Afghanistan at that point and very little of the machinations of the local power brokers. The ODAs had expected to arrive to battle organized al-Qaeda and Taliban resistance but instead encountered Afghan militias that would change sides at the drop of a hat and betray their former comrades for a cash bribe. As they made their way through unknown villages with unknown allegiances, the ODAs were told to "smile and wave with one hand and grip your weapon tight with the other, ready to fire."

Tora Bora and *Anaconda*

Intelligence developed by the CIA's Jawbreaker teams placed bin Laden in Jalalabad and described al-Qaeda fighters moving through the city, heading for the mountainous border with Pakistan. The Jawbreaker commander described the situation in an interview several years later:

Special Forces medics treat an injured Afghan civilian. Note the unusual knife scabbard worn attached to the pistol drop holster of the Green Beret in the Polartec jacket to the left. (USASOC)

… in mid-November the capital, Kabul collapses. I immediately learn that bin Laden has fled into Nangarhar Province, Southeastern Afghanistan. I send an eight-man team into a Province, which is in complete chaos. There are company sized Chechen elements moving around, al-Qaeda, Taliban. And I sit down with my deputy and he and seven others link up with a warlord … An Afghan warlord, not a member of the Northern Alliance.

We moved with him down to the mountains, we had learned that bin Laden was up in the mountains. I put a four-man team up onto a mountain with ten Afghan guides and they got over the mother lode of al-Qaeda. Bin Laden had fallen back with about a thousand people. They used the laser designator that they have and a radio and they call in air strikes relentlessly for 56 hours that begins the battle of Tora Bora.

A joint CIA/Delta Force team had arrived in the Spin Ghar (White Dust) Mountains in the first week of December and located evidence of large numbers of foreign al-Qaeda fighters inhabiting the mountains. One CIA-led element established an observation post over an al-Qaeda-held village near Tora Bora and began to call in air strikes. The Tora Bora Mountains, known as Black Dust, had a long association with al-Qaeda. Bin Laden had used the area as a base of operations during the Soviet–Afghan War and had curried favor with the local population by making donations to each family. Apparently one of the first meetings that would eventually result in

A newly donated police vehicle clearly given by Germany and manned by what would become the Afghan National Police. Note their communist-style uniforms and rather unfortunate licence plate number. (JZW)

the September 11 terrorist attacks was conducted within the shadow of Tora Bora.

The CIA intelligence convinced Colonel Mulholland to dispatch a Special Forces ODA to Tora Bora. Former Delta Force commander "Dalton Fury" writes that Mulholland wanted his men to wear "US military uniforms, ostensibly to prevent friendly-fire incidents … The men of 5th Group determined that they could meet the intent of their commander's orders by wearing US desert tan uniform pants, but everything else came out of an Afghan wardrobe. They had to blend in to have any hope of success." Mulholland placed an additional restriction on the Green Berets – they were authorized only to conduct TGO (Terminal Guidance Operations) and were not allowed to go forward hunting al-Qaeda. TGO was military shorthand for calling in airstrikes using their radios and SOFLAM laser markers.

ODA 572 operating under the call sign Cobra 25 was eventually sent forward to Tora Bora and established an observation post high above the Milawa Valley that bordered Pakistan and Tora Bora. The team carried with it pieces of rubble from the Twin Towers. Among their first tasks was burying a piece of rubble from the Towers at Tora Bora and erecting a simple plaque with an inscription memorializing the FDNY and NYPD losses in New York.

With a CIA down payment of a quarter of a million dollars on the table, the compliance and somewhat questionable assistance of the local AMF commanders was secured under the command of Eastern Alliance General Hazret Ali, a long-time CIA asset. His AMF had been equipped from US-supplied stocks and his militiamen now wore US woodland pattern cold-weather jackets and carried AKs from CIA warehouses (the AMF were told not to wear turbans as a friendly fire countermeasure – the Taliban traditionally wore black turbans – and instead donned Afghan *pakol* hats). A second Afghan warlord, Haji Zaman Ghamshareek, was also added to the CIA's payroll for the mission. Neither of the warlords was known by the Special Forces men and their pedigrees remain untested.

Tora Bora was a time-sensitive target. If they did not attack in December, it would be several months until the weather

What appears to be a Soviet KPV 14.5mm anti-aircraft cannon recovered during a Special Forces raid on a Taliban weapons cache based on locally gathered intelligence. Behind the cannon is a modified cargo HMMWV with another Green Beret maintaining security on the vehicle. (JZW)

Two recently arrived Green Berets – evidenced by the lack of facial hair. Both wear the then-fashionable drop holsters and have eschewed their body armor as many of the early ODAs did. The operator on the left appears to have mounted an Aimpoint "red dot" sight unusually forward on his M4A1's foregrip. (USASOC)

enabled them to do so again. Several plans were sent up the increasingly risk-averse chain of command. A plan to insert small teams of American operators high on the peaks on the Pakistan side of the border to call in air strikes on any enemy that managed to escape was denied. Another request, to use air-dropped Gator anti-personnel mines, was also denied. Finally the head of the CIA team made an impassioned plea to make use of the Rangers, who were sitting in nearby Bagram on standby, as a blocking force in the mountain passes. This too was denied.

The Green Berets established an observation post on the eastern flank of the mountain with half of the ODA while the other half relieved the joint CIA/JSOC team's position. Delta Force snipers, trained as ground FACs, were dispatched to partner up with the teams. Delta had also been given operational command of the ODA, which understandably rankled the Special Forces men, but they got on with their job, marking targets for destruction from the air. The AMF were wary of allowing the Americans forward as they were considered a valuable revenue source that senior militia commanders did not want to see killed.

The AMF were simply not performing and would fall back each night, ceding captured ground back to al-Qaeda. On December 12, Haji Zaman Ghamshareek announced that al-Qaeda had surrendered and was working out the exact terms of the agreement to lay down its arms. Ghamshareek told the Americans that they could not attack while the negotiations continued. Sensing that the surrender was a sham, the Americans proceeded back up the mountain until they were stopped by some 80-odd militiamen aiming their AKs at them.

After some terse negotiations, the AMF eventually agreed to allow the operators to advance up past the two Green Beret observation posts. A request was made to their headquarters for several of the Green Berets to accompany the AMF further up the mountain to act as ground FACs. Inexplicably, Task Force Dagger denied this request and the Green Berets withdrew, the detachment commander relieved of his command for apparently defying operational restrictions placed on the ODA. This, along

G | **ANOTHER WAR, ANOTHER ROLE – DESERT MOBILITY**

All too soon, the men of the 5th Special Forces Group were ordered back to Fort Bragg to prepare for another war, what would become known as Operation *Iraqi Freedom* (OIF). Many left with grave misgivings as they felt the job was not yet complete in Afghanistan and they had developed strong ties with their G-Chiefs, ties that might well have helped Afghanistan prosper rather than wither and descend into a vicious insurgency.

These men, again from our fictional ODA, are preparing for their future warfighting role in the deserts of western Iraq by conducting specialist mobility training with their ground mobility vehicles or GMVs. The GMV was based on the standard HMMWV and was developed from the desert mobility vehicles or Dumvees used for the first time in Iraq during Operation *Desert Storm*. Each GMV is extensively refitted for long-range patrolling and includes integrated satellite communications, Blue Force Tracker and increased cargo capacity. The vehicles also have an offensive punch with mounted .50-cal M2 heavy machine guns, 40mm Mk 19 and later Mk 47 automatic grenade launchers and 7.62mm M240B medium machine guns.

2001 US Department of Defense map of Afghanistan. (DOD)

with losing operational command to Delta, was demoralizing for the men of the Special Forces. These types of decisions would become more commonplace only as staff headquarters and "Big Army thinking" arrived from the United States.

Later a second team, ODA 561, was sent in to conduct SSEs alongside ODA 572 – this was a painstaking and often grisly task as the Green Berets sifted through the rubble of caves struck by aerial bombs, looking for intelligence or the DNA of the al-Qaeda leader. Most of the caves were small natural affairs in the rock walls of the mountains – not the vast James Bond-style complexes reported in the media at the time. Some of the larger caverns had been extended during the Soviet–Afghan War – some by bin Laden's men – and reinforced to hold ammunition stockpiles. Bin Laden's last transmission had been intercepted on December 14, 2001 and he escaped into Pakistan soon after. He was eventually and famously killed nearly ten years later in Abbottabad by a Navy Special Mission Unit in May 2011.

After the disappointment and frustration of Tora Bora, several ODAs from the 5th and 3rd Special Forces Groups became involved in what would be the largest and most decisive operation of the Afghan war to date. Operation *Anaconda* was planned based on both CIA and ground reconnaissance conducted by ODA 594 and JSOC elements of the Lower Shah-i-Khot Valley, a mountainous area of eastern Afghanistan bordering Pakistan. The intelligence picture seemed to indicate that al-Qaeda remnants were using the valley as a safe area. Colonel Mulholland worked with the commanders of the 10th Mountain and 101st Airborne Divisions to develop a plan of attack.

The plan was relatively straightforward and placed the men of the Special Forces firmly as the main effort. A force element of some five hundred AMF, with ODAs 594 and 372 in support, would constitute Task Force Hammer and enter the western approach to the valley to flush out the enemy. Task Force Anvil, split into two subordinate units composed of ODA 542 and ODA 381 with some 300–500 AMF, would man blocking positions to the south, while ODA 571 and ODA 392 would do likewise in the east with 500 AMF to preclude any escape into Pakistan. A third force, Task Force Rakkasan, would air-assault by helicopter into the eastern end of the valley itself to establish further blocking positions. Coalition and American SOF units would be deployed on the peaks to act as observation posts and to guide in close air support.

The operation launched on March 2, 2002 and immediately ran into challenges. Several AMF vehicles broke down during Task Force Hammer's approach and all light discipline was lost when some of the confused Afghan drivers turned on their headlights. A further truck rolled over in the darkness, injuring a number of AMF. Soon after, these challenges turned to tragedy when a circling AC-130 misidentified part of the AMF column as enemy and engaged an American HMMWV killing a Green Beret Warrant Officer and two Afghans and wounding several more. This delayed the advance of Task Force Hammer even further. A planned aerial bombardment of suspected al-Qaeda positions at the entrance to the valley then failed to materialize, leaving the AMF demoralized. The proverbial straw that broke the camel's back was an al-Qaeda mortar barrage that effectively shattered the Afghans' cohesion. After a hurried conversation with Mulholland, the ODAs and their Afghans pulled back to their start point in Gardez.

The American air assault went in as planned, thankfully without the loss of any helicopters, but the men of Task Force Rakkasan were immediately pinned down on the valley floor by enemy fire from the heights. The intelligence had been incorrect – the enemy was not in the villages in the valley but hidden in caves on the steep sides of the valley. ODA 563 had inserted with the 101st Airborne and quickly split into sub-units to support the conventional forces. Eventually the surrounded Americans were withdrawn during the next night. A crash-landed MH-47 on a mountaintop called Takur Ghar diverted extensive resources to save firstly a missing SEAL and then both a SEAL reconnaissance team that returned to rescue him and a Ranger QRF that landed to reinforce the SEALs.

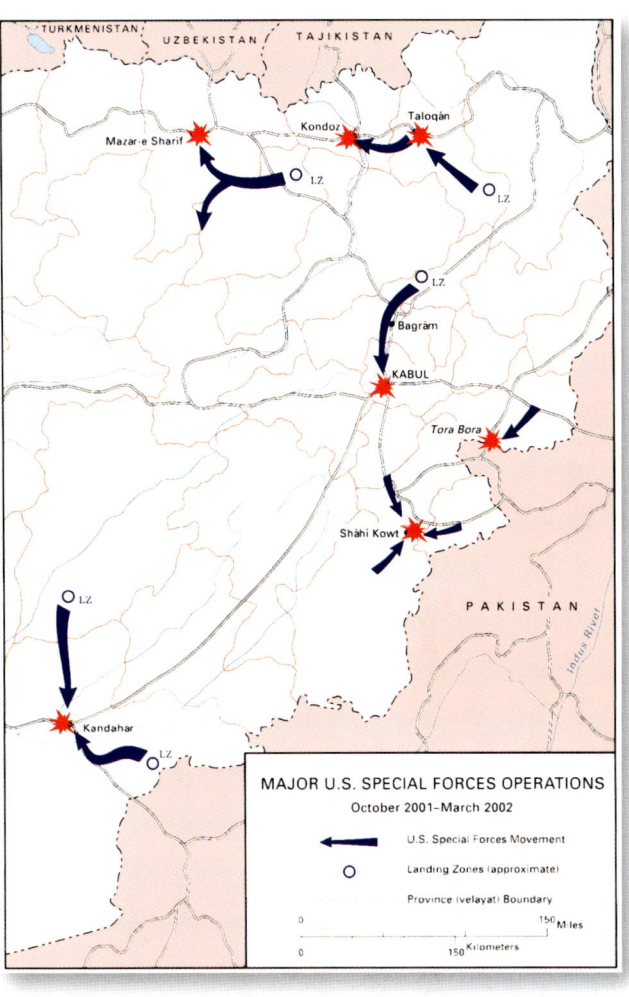

A US Department of Defense map detailing Army Special Forces operations including the major helicopter landing zones. (DOD)

MAJOR U.S. SPECIAL FORCES OPERATIONS
October 2001–March 2002

U.S. Special Forces Movement
Landing Zones (approximate)
Province (velayat) Boundary

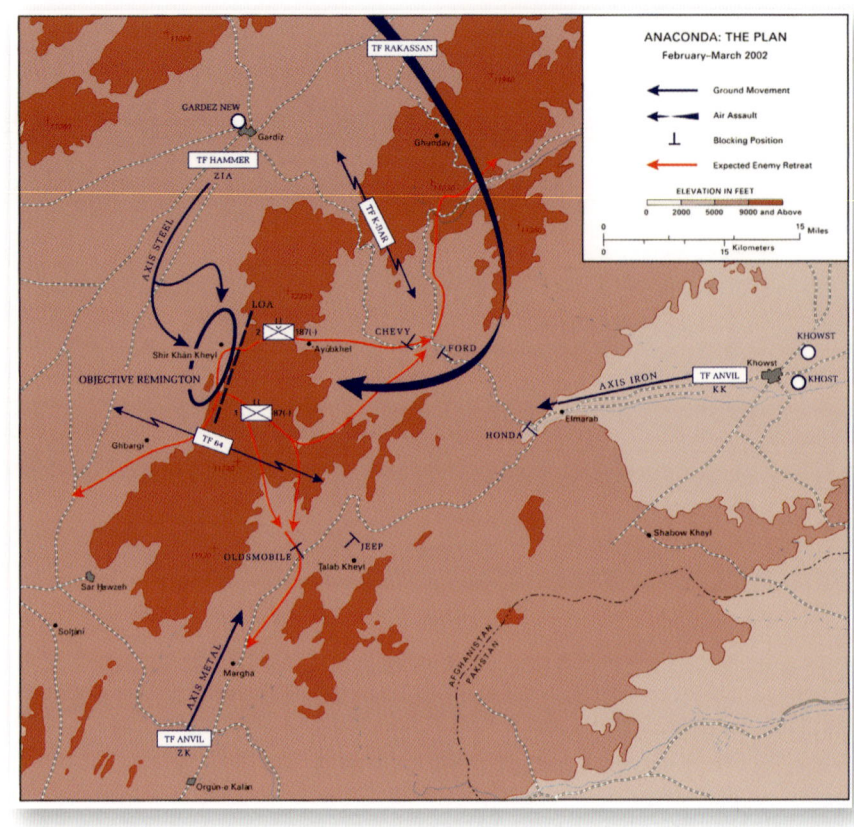

A US Department of Defense map showing the original plan for Operation *Anaconda* – note the original mission for the Special Forces-led Task Force Hammer which ended in tragedy after an AC-130 mistakenly engaged them, killing a number of AMF and Green Beret Chief Warrant Officer Stanley Harriman. This incident, along with more ferocious opposition than expected and much less than expected preparatory air bombardments, prematurely ended the advance of Task Force Hammer with the AMF retreating back to Gardez. (DOD)

Eventually Task Force Hammer returned to the fight and established fire support positions and checkpoints. Other AMF under the direction of ODAs 394, 372 and 594 entered the northern end of the valley on March 6, but the enemy had largely fled. *Anaconda* was declared a success and although it certainly resulted in the killing of a large number of enemy, it was largely bittersweet for the Green Berets. What had begun as a Special Forces-led operation was, by necessity, taken over by the conventional forces of Task Force Rakkasan. The ODAs had again, like at Tora Bora, experienced the intense rivalries between competing warlords and the often fragile morale of the AMF.

By April 2002, 5th Group was on its way back to Fort Bragg to begin preparations for the invasion of Iraq. A battalion of the 3rd Special Forces Group, along with elements from the 7th Special Forces Group and the National Guard's 19th Special Forces Group, replaced them in Afghanistan. Over the following years, as the insurgency in Iraq burgeoned, Operation *Enduring Freedom* would come to rely largely on the men of the two National Guard Special Forces Groups to continue the fight.

The departure of the 5th Special Forces Group was not the only loss. Strategic reconnaissance assets from JSOC and the CIA were refocused on Iraq and the Predator UAV fleet was re-tasked to the Middle East. Gary Schroen of the CIA Jawbreaker teams witnessed this loss of essential assets first

A small team of Green Berets search through the shattered remains of an al-Qaeda bunker in the Shahikot Valley post Operation *Anaconda* – note the American in the center wearing the *pakol* appears to be carrying an AK indicating his probable employment by the CIA. (USASOC)

hand "... the Special Forces Group was being pulled out to refit and get ready for Iraq. It was clear that the kind of guys that I think a lot of us believed was essential – US military personnel with special operations capabilities – was being pulled away."

What of our fictional ODA, Copperhead Zero One? They too would have been unceremoniously dispatched back to North Carolina to begin preparations for operations in Iraq. As one ODA master sergeant explained:

> We were given notification of there being aircraft for us and in two hours be on it. They extended it; we had about six hours to pack everything up and get on an aircraft and fly out ... Because we'd left on such short notice, we sent approximately half the team back in to say good bye to [General] Dostum. Dostum was quite upset with our leaving. Probably because of the way it happened, and partly because we had gone through a lot of fighting together. He wasn't quite ready for us to leave.

Along with the withdrawal of mission critical assets, the nature of the war was beginning to change as conventional commanders assumed responsibility for the theater. The free-wheeling innovation of those few months in late 2001 that dismantled the Taliban regime was replaced by a risk-averse culture that largely stymied unconventional thinking, and with it Unconventional Warfare. As one operator commented in 2002, "We now need a CONOPS to leave the gate." (A CONOPS is a concept of operations document that spells out a proposed operation in minute detail.) This was made worse by the inter-service rivalry of a military that had not been on a war footing for many years.

In mid-2002, a CIA team developed apparently reliable intelligence on the whereabouts of Taliban leader Mullah Omar. A National Guard ODA

The experiences of the Special Forces in Afghanistan resulted in a new Mountaineering Program that includes climbing, rope, and rappelling techniques along with the use of pack animals and horse-riding. (US Army photograph by SSG Russell Lee Klika)

An Air Force Combat Controller watches in satisfaction as another airstrike hits Taliban positions. Note the Green Beret in the Afghan pakol hat to the right using the SOFLAM laser designator. In the foreground is a SATCOM radio antennae array. (US Army)

was located nearby and could have conducted a raid to capture or kill him, but the ODA was overlooked or ignored in the turf war between different branches of the US military. The intelligence was sent to Task Force 11 (formerly Task Force Sword), the designated high-value target force, but they did not arrive in time and the target escaped US custody. This was yet another example of the inter-service rivalry and petty squabbling which characterized US special operations in Afghanistan in the years immediately following the overthrow of the Taliban.

The legend of the horse soldiers even crops up in Army recruiting including this recent print advertisement for Army Special Forces. (USASOC)

EXPERIENCE OF BATTLE

From their first infiltration into Afghanistan until after the fall of the final strategic city, Kandahar, the Special Forces had largely fought their own war on their own terms. Experts at unconventional warfare, the Green Berets drew on their extensive training and operational experience dating back to Vietnam to develop the situation on the ground in an extremely fluid and unpredictable environment.

They succeeded for several reasons. Principally, they were allowed to prosecute the campaign on their own terms and using their unique strengths. No other entity within the US military could have done what the Green Berets managed – entering a foreign country, linking up with G-Chiefs of largely unknown provenance, convincing those warlords that with American help they could defeat the Taliban, and eventually going to war alongside those warlords and their militia, often on horseback as "21st-century cavalry." Their Unconventional Warfare model worked.

The devastating might of American air power also contributed in no small way. US Navy, Marine Air Wing and Air Force aircraft, joined by the Royal Air Force, rewrote the close air support manual. The opening months of the Afghan war saw the first use of a Predator UAV in direct support of troops in contact and attached Combat Controllers guided in GPS and laser-guided bombs from B-52 and B-1B strategic bombers, as they were some of the only aircraft that had the fuel capacity to loiter over the remote battle space of Afghanistan.

Technology on the ground also played a huge part in the Green Berets' success. The SOFLAM laser designator has justifiably become legendary. It allowed the ODAs to direct bombs from the sky with accuracy that inspired

The America's Response monument in New York City, opposite 1 World Trade Center. Dedicated on November 11, 2011 by Lieutenant-General John Mulholland, it sports the Green Beret's motto – *De Oppresso Liber* (To liberate the oppressed). (USASOC)

53

A Green Beret conducts a principles of marksmanship training session with a group of AMF. (JZW)

confidence from their Afghan warlord allies. The SOFLAM allowed the Americans to keep their promises. The fact that the majority of ordnance being dropped was overwhelmingly "smart" with GPS, TV or laser guidance meant that the risk of collateral damage or fratricide that could have threatened fragile new alliances was reduced, but as we have seen, it can never be totally discounted.

The Green Berets' access to incredibly accurate and powerful airpower meant that the war was largely fought at a distance through the optics of a SOFLAM. It was rare for the ODAs to be involved in situations that required

A Special Forces Weapons Sergeant zeroing his camouflage-painted M24 sniper rifle. Note the empty M249 SAW drum at his right elbow and spotting scope to his left. He wears a commercially purchased Camelbak hydration system. (JZW)

Green Berets, visible on the top right, sit down for a traditional meal with local elders and police. The Afghans eat only with their right hands, considering the left unclean, and all serve themselves from communal plates of rice, chicken, goat, salad, and flatbread, all washed down with locally produced soft drinks or sweet chai (tea). (JZW)

the use of their personal weapons, although these situations did occasionally occur. In the later months, as Direct Action missions increased so too did the occurrence of firefights. After 2002, Special Forces began to concentrate on the Direct Action mission almost to the exclusion of their other skills, a situation that was only partly reversed from 2010 with the Village Stability Operations initiative in Afghanistan where Special Forces went back to Unconventional Warfare and Foreign Internal Defense roots.

The experience of fighting with the Afghans was unique. The individual Afghan could be a well-motivated and enthusiastic soldier if well led, although

A Special Forces team visits a local village to discuss civil development projects in early 2002. The stark difference in posture and equipment compared with more recent operations is illuminating. The Green Berets do not wear body armor or helmets and carry their M4A1s slung – unthinkable even a few years later in most of Afghanistan. (JZW)

the Afghan way of war took some getting used to. Like many tribal societies, conflict was more about bluff, intimidation and face-saving than body counts. The ODAs witnessed this first hand, as the capitulation of key cities was accomplished as much through negotiation as firepower. The Afghans responded well to the Americans once they understood what the ODAs (and the CIA) could bring to the table. One thing that the Afghans could never be was fully trusted – culturally, shifting allegiances are not dishonorable but an accepted part of conducting warfare.

As noted earlier, after the fall of Kandahar, the men of the ODAs began to feel the impact of the arrival of "Big Army" – conventional forces with

THE TOOLS OF WAR – FROM SUPPRESSIVE TO SURGICAL

Along with their personal small arms like the M4A1 SOPMOD carbine and the Mk 12 SPR, the ODAs also deployed into Afghanistan with a range of heavy weapons. The operator himself is shown in typical two-piece Afghan dress called the *shalwar kameez*. He wears a modified Chi-Com magazine chest rig and carries a Claymore bag slung to his side; these were often used as dump pouches to drop expended magazines into. His weapon is the 5.56 x 45mm M4A1 SOPMOD equipped with a Trijicon ACOG optic, vertical foregrip and Knights Quick Detachable suppressor.

Displayed on the page around him are the .50 M82A1 (later type classed as the M107) Special Application Scoped Rifle (SASR) at the top (**1**); the 7.62 x 51mm M24 Sniper Weapon System (SWS) on the far left (**2**); the 7.62 x 51mm Mk 11 Mod 0 Special Purpose Rifle next to the M24 (**3**); the 7.62 x 51mm M240B medium machine gun on the right next to the figure (**4**) and the FGM-148 Javelin Anti-Tank Guided Missile at the bottom of the page (**5**). To the right of the M240B is illustrated a small arms curiosity of the Afghan war– the Knights Armament Company SR-47 in 7.62 x 39mm Soviet (**6**). The M82A1/M107 SASR, the M24 SWS and the Mk 11 Mod 0 all serve as long-range sniping platforms, although each for specific requirements. The M82A1/M107 enjoys an extended range beyond 1,800m and fires the massive .50-cal. round, able to engage light armour and soft-skinned vehicles with ease. The M24 is a robust bolt-action design based on the civilian Remington 700, accurate beyond 800m and at the time of the commencement of operations in Afghanistan, was the standard US Army sniper rifle. The Mk 11 Mod 0 was a relative newcomer along with the Mk 12 SPR and was based on the earlier Knights SR-25, designed for circumstances where rapid follow-on shots, or the ability to be used as an assault rifle, were more important than the pinpoint accuracy of the bolt-action M24.

Based upon the famous FN MAG58, the belt-fed M240B served as the Special Forces' primary machine gun in Afghanistan, deploying mounted in GMVs and Toyota pick-ups, on its tripod in a sustained fire role at Fire Bases and, with its standard bipod, out on the ground during raids and ambushes. Like its British cousin the L7A2 GPMG, the M240B commands well-earned respect on the battlefield. The 5.56mm M249 SAW was also commonly carried due to its lighter weight and portability, in particular the then recently developed SOCOM version, the Mk 46 Mod 0.

The FGM-148, more commonly referred to as simply the Javelin, is a true fire-and-forget missile system with a top-attack mode that proved immensely valuable when attacking Taliban compounds and fighting positions. Simply move the electronic reticule gates in the sight around the target, hold them in place until you hear the tone and you are locked on. Once launched, the Javelin will actually follow targets that move such as Taliban technicals. Its Command Launch Unit (CLU) also proved popular as a superb thermal day or night sight. The ODAs also carried a large number of both M136 (AT4) and M72 light anti-tank rockets to engage Taliban and al-Qaeda strongpoints and bunkers.

Finally, the KAC SR-47 is shown with a Picatinny rail kit, EO Tech sight and suppressor fitted. Perhaps the most expensive rifle produced in recent memory, the SR-47 was born from a request from SOCOM for an M4 carbine that could accept AK47 magazines and that fired the Russian 7.62x39mm round. The thinking behind the request was that ODAs may find themselves at the extreme end of the resupply chain in Afghanistan and may be better served with a weapon that could be replenished from captured enemy stocks. Only seven of this experimental weapon were hand-manufactured at a reported prototype cost of over one million dollars. Six were delivered to SOCOM but what became of them is unknown. No further orders were received either for the SR-47 or a proposed variant chambering the AK-74's 5.45 x 39mm round.

1

2   3   4

                                                              6

5

conventional ways of operating. What had been a Special Forces main effort would now be taken over by the often slow-moving and risk-averse military bureaucracy. It was not just conventional forces that caused this situation – as forward headquarters from the Army Special Operations Command deployed into Afghanistan, the ODAs experienced their every move being questioned and evaluated with an inevitable impact on their operations.

AFTERMATH OF BATTLE: A MISSED OPPORTUNITY AND THE BIRTH OF A MODERN LEGEND

As mentioned, during 2002 the focus was no longer on Afghanistan but on the impending operations in Iraq in support of what would become known as Operation *Iraqi Freedom*. The Green Berets would play a significant part in that war. ODAs from the 10th Special Forces Group would penetrate into Northern Iraq months before hostilities began, working alongside their Peshmerga allies (and in much the same way as the Special Forces advisers are operating with the Kurds in stemming the onslaught of Islamic State); others from the 5th Special Forces Group would conduct long-range special reconnaissance missions far ahead of the advancing Coalition armies. Later they would become key enablers in training a new Iraqi Army able to do battle in an increasingly complex counter-insurgency.

Despite these Special Forces successes in Iraq, the loss of focus on Afghanistan allowed the Taliban to slowly and carefully rebuild in the tribal borderlands of Pakistan and in the largely ungoverned southern provinces of Afghanistan. The continuing Special Forces presence was small – there were outlying ODAs that could exert some local influence but this was far from a

A Special Forces operator maintains security behind an M2 .50-cal mounted upon a HMMWV while a *shura* is conducted inside the village – see the noticeboard from the local governor in front of the vehicle. *Shuras* are required firstly to gain the trust of the village elders and later to agree any decisions regarding security or civil affairs projects. (JZW)

A Special Forces patrol negotiates a mountain trail somewhere in Eastern Afghanistan. The width and condition of these trails often negated the use of the wider and heavier HMMWV in favor of the Toyota pick-up truck. (JZW)

concerted ink-blot counter-insurgency approach. The Taliban gained ground in its traditional heartlands in Kandahar and Helmand and when, in 2006, the International Security Assistance Force (ISAF) attempted to expand the influence of the Afghan central government, a vicious insurgency ensued.

The United States slowly re-entered Afghanistan in greater numbers, but sent their SOF assets on missions to degrade insurgent leadership and logistical capability. It was not until the Iraq Surge was completed and withdrawal from Iraq largely accomplished that significant numbers of Army Special Forces returned to Afghanistan. The period in 2002 following the fall of the Taliban is often regarded as the "golden hour" for Afghanistan when Western forces had enough goodwill and popular support to stabilize Afghanistan. Instead, assets were diverted and the impoverished nation continues to struggle today while Western forces have largely been withdrawn.

The "horse soldiers" of the 5th and 3rd Special Forces Groups in those final months of 2001 have also left an indelible cultural imprint both within the military and on the larger public consciousness. Linda Robinson described it well when she wrote, "The Special Forces, allied with 18th century style fighters on the ground and a powerful 21st century air force overhead, had seized the country's imagination."

Within the US military, the Green Beret has again become synonymous with unconventional warfare. Unlike the Navy SEALs who actively court and receive the lion's share of the spotlight, the Green Berets have continued to be the true "Quiet Professionals," shunning the publicity and maintaining a low profile. With the shift away from Direct Action, the Army Special Forces are once more focusing on their language and cultural skills. That emphasis has resulted in the 2014 raising of a fourth battalion within each Special Forces Group.

These new battalions will be focused purely on Foreign Internal Defense and Unconventional Warfare to address what the Pentagon is now terming "hybrid warfare" of the type seen recently in the Ukraine, with the Russian government ostensibly supporting insurgents, covertly deploying their own

Deployed alongside the ODAs and the Civil Affairs teams were the Psychological Operations Detachments known as PSYOPS. They normally used custom HMMWVs mounting loud speakers to impart their messages, but, in the early days of the Afghan campaign, vehicles such as this locally procured Toyota were jury-rigged with speakers. (JZW)

SOF and, finally, deploying Russian conventional forces, albeit in a clandestine manner. It will also increasingly become the model in the war against so-called Islamic State in Iraq and Syria and jihadist insurgencies across Africa and the Middle East.

The Marine Corps Special Operations Command (MARSOC) has been copying the ODA formula, understanding that Foreign Internal Defense and Unconventional Warfare will be a large part of the future of special operations. The MARSOC Raider Teams are even organized in a similar manner to Army ODAs with the ability to split into two sub-units and a headquarters element. MARSOC has also recognized the power of languages and places a high importance on this phase of training.

The image of the bearded Special Forces soldier has undoubtedly also crept into the cultural Zeitgeist. Console video games such as *Medal of Honor* and *Call of Duty: Modern Warfare* feature Green Beret types, personified by their exotic weapons and facial hair. A similar image has even been used in US Army recruiting. The print advert shows a soldier dressed in a mix of Afghan and military clothing with the accompanying tagline "Green Berets Don't Always Wear a Green Beret."

Several accomplished books have been published, among them Doug Stanton's *Horse Soldiers* and Eric Blehm's *The Only Thing Worth Dying For.* Stanton's work has been optioned by Hollywood and is unlikely to be the only Green Beret movie to reach our screens. A statue has even been erected near to Ground Zero in New York City called the America's Response Monument depicting a mounted Green Beret from the early weeks of the Afghan campaign. Former Colonel, now Lieutenant-General, John Mulholland was on hand at its dedication ceremony on November 11, 2011.

BIBLIOGRAPHY

US Army Field Manual ADRP 3-05 Special Operations

Berntsen, Gary and Pezzullo, Ralph, *Jawbreaker: The attack on bin Laden and al-Qaeda; A personal account by CIA's key field commander* (New York, Crown, 2005)

Blehm, Eric, *The Only Thing Worth Dying For: How Eleven Green Berets Forged A New Afghanistan* (New York, Harper Collins, 2010)

Briscoe, Charles H.; Kiper, Richard L., Schroeder, James A.; and Sepp, Kalev I., *Weapon of Choice US Army Special Operation Forces in Afghanistan* (Fort Leavenworth, Combat Studies Press, 2003)

Call, Steve, *Danger Close: Tactical Air Controllers in Afghanistan and Iraq* (College Station, Texas University Press, 2007)

Camp, Dick, *Boots on the Ground: The fight to liberate Afghanistan from al-Qaeda and the Taliban 2001–2002* (Minneapolis, Zenith Press, 2011)

Couch, Dick, *Chosen Soldier; the making of a Special Forces Warrior* (New York, Three Rivers Press, 2007)

Fury, Dalton, *Kill Bin Laden: A Delta Force Commander's Account of the Hunt for the World's Most Wanted Man* (New York, St Martin's Press, 2008)

Grau, Lester W., and Billingsley, Dodge, *Operation Anaconda: America's First Major Battle in Afghanistan* (Kansas, University Press of Kansas, 2011)

Naylor, Sean, *Not a Good Day to Die: The Untold Story of Operation Anaconda* (New York, Berkley, 2005)

Robinson, Linda, *Masters of Chaos: The Secret History of the Special Forces* (New York, Public Affairs, 2004)

Schroen, Gary, *First In: An Insider's Account of How the CIA Spearheaded the War on Terror in Afghanistan* (New York, Presidio, 2005)

Stanton, Doug, *Horse Soldiers: A True Story of Modern War* (New York, Scribner, 2009)

GLOSSARY

ACOG	Advanced Combat Optical Gunsight
AIA	Afghan Interim Authority
AMF	Afghan Militia Forces/Fighters
ARSOF	Army Special Operations Forces
ATV	All Terrain Vehicle (a quad bike)
BALCS	Ballistic Armor Load Carrying System
BDU	Battle Dress Utility (camouflage fatigues)
buzkashi	a traditional Afghan sport on horseback
CENTCOM	US Central Command (in charge of Afghan theater)
CCT	US Air Force Combat Controller
COIN	Counter-Insurgency
CQB	Close-Quarter Battle
CSAR	Combat Search and Rescue
CT	Counterterrorism
DA	Direct Action: quick-duration strikes to seize, capture, recover or destroy enemy weapons and information or to recover personnel or material
DAP	Direct Action Penetrator (a special operations gunship version of the MH-60 helicopter)
DCU	Desert Camouflage Uniform
DOD	US Department of Defense
ECW	Extreme Cold Weather (clothing)
EPW	Enemy Prisoner (of) War
FARC	Fuerzas Armadas Revolucionarias de Colombia (Colombian insurgency)
FDNY	Fire Department, City of New York
FID	Foreign Internal Defense: the task of establishing, training and mentoring allied nations' militaries to counter an insurgent or guerrilla threat
FMLN	Frente Farabundo Martí para la Liberación Nacional (Salvadorian insurgency)
G-Chief	local-national guerilla leader
G-FACs	Ground Forward Air Controller
GMV	Ground Mobility Vehicle (a Special Forces modified HMMWV)
HALO	High-Altitude Low-Opening, also known as military free fall parachuting
HESCO	collapsible dirt-filled fortifications common on Coalition bases
HMMWV	High Mobility Multipurpose Wheeled Vehicle
Jedburgh Team	WWII era special operations teams that deployed behind enemy lines to conduct unconventional warfare
jihad	a holy war undertaken by Muslims against unbelievers
JSOC	Joint Special Operations Command
KAC	Knight Armament Corporation
MBITR	Multiband Inter/Intra Team Radio
MICH	Modular Integrated Communications Helmet
MOLLE	Modular Lightweight Load (carrying) Equipment
MOS	Military Occupational Specialty

mujahid	an Islamic holy warrior
NALT	CIA Northern Alliance Liaison Team
NBC	Nuclear, Biological Chemical
NGO	Non-Governmental Organization
NYPD	New York City Police Department
ODA	Operational Detachment Alpha, also known as an A-Team
ODB	Operational Detachment Bravo; the command and control element for a Special Forces Company
ODC	Operational Detachment Charlie; the command and control element for a Special Forces Battalion
OEF	Operation *Enduring Freedom*
pakol	Afghan flat-topped cap
PLGR	Precision Lightweight GPS Receiver
PSYOPS	Psychological Operations
QRF	Quick Reaction Force
Robin Sage	the final field exercise of the Special Forces Qualification Course
SAD	CIA Special Activities Division
SAW	Squad Automatic Weapon (the M249 or Minimi)
SBS	UK Special Boat Service
SFAS	Special Forces Assessment and Selection: a pre-selection course to filter potential Green Berets
shalwar kameez	traditional matching baggy top and trousers worn by most Afghan males
shemagh	scarf worn to protect against dust storms
shura	meeting with Afghan elders or tribal leaders
SOAR	160th Special Operations Aviation Regiment
SOCOM	US Special Operations Command
SOF	Special Operations Forces
SOFLAM	Special Operations Forces Laser Acquisition Marker
SOPMOD	Special Operations Peculiar Modification
SPEAR	Special Operations Forces Equipment Advanced Requirements
SPR	Special Purpose Rifle (Mk 12, Mod 0)
SSE	Sensitive Site Exploitation
UAV	Unmanned Aerial Vehicle (drone)
UW	unconventional warfare: used to attempt to raise a guerrilla force in a hostile host nation to act against an oppressive regime that is hostile to United States interests

INDEX

Figures in **bold** refer to illustrations.